PRAISE FROM GUIDANCE COUNSELORS
AND FAMILY THERAPISTS FOR

HOW TO LIVE WITH YOUR TEENAGER

"Invaluable . . . practical, workable, down to earth."
Dr. Thomas F. Dignam
Executive Director
Sunset Hills Family Counseling Center

"The authors have taken some highly valid principles and presented them in a comprehensive fashion that the typical parent can understand quite readily."
Dr. Everett L. Jacobson
President
Southern California Psychotherapy

"A sensible format for nurturing the most delicate time in everyone's life."
Bill Caughron, M.A.
Marriage, Family, and Child Counselor

"An opportunity to share concerns, increase communication and improve understanding. DON'T MISS IT!"
B. J. Meyers, M.S., M.F.C.C
High School Guidance Counselor

HOW TO LIVE WITH YOUR TEENAGER

A Survivor's Handbook for Parents

Peter H. Buntman, M.S.W., ACSW

Eleanor M. Saris, M.E.D.

BALLANTINE BOOKS • NEW YORK

Copyright © 1979 by THE BIRCH TREE PRESS

Excerpt of six lines from "On Children" (on page 121) reprinted from THE PROPHET, by Kahlil Gibran, with permission of the publisher, Alfred A. Knopf, Inc. Copyright 1923 by Kahlil Gibran; renewal copyright 1951 by Administrators C.T.A. of Kahlil Gibran Estate, and Mary G. Gibran.

Graph on page 14, Chapter 2, is reprinted with permission of Fred Streit, Ed.D from "PARENTS AND PROBLEMS: Through the Eyes of Youth."

Library of Congress Catalog Card Number: 79-98287

ISBN 0-345-33428-0

This edition published by arrangement with The Birch Tree Press

Printed in Canada

First Ballantine Books Edition: April 1982
Eleventh Printing: August 1991

Acknowledgments

To acknowledge all the people—parents, teenagers, therapists and friends—who helped inspire and spark our creativity would take many pages.

However, we wish to especially acknowledge the following therapists who gave invaluable contributions to us: their ideas, their feedback, their support. Each of them took time from their private practice to share with us their insight and knowledge gained over the years working with teenagers and their families. We are indebted to:

Marilyn Cohen, M.S.W., LCSW
Merv Cooper, M.S.W., LCSW
Barbara Henry, M.S.W., LCSW
Everett Jacobson, Ph.D.
Julianna de Bruyn Kops, M.S.W., LCSW
David Wenner, M.S.W.

A very special acknowledgment to: Merv Cooper, M.S.W., LCSW, Executive Director of the Southern California Psychotherapy Association, who gave unstintingly of his time, talent and insight, and above all, his constructive editing. He gave us his love, his criticism, and his support. Thank you, dear friend.

To Mary Kay Konfal, a very special "thank you" for your support and encouragement.

Table of Contents

*skill. Sometimes you can get stuck choosing
the right word—these lists can help you
choose just the right word to describe what
you're feeling.)*

Dedication

To our friends and colleagues across the country who are actively involved in the development and growth of local Institutes for Adolescent Studies throughout the country.

To the parents and teenagers who shared with us their pain, their problems and their struggles and in so doing helped us learn from them.

To Jamie, Jason, Elena, Elnora and hundreds of other teenagers whose help and guidance we sought and received tenfold.

We thank you all.

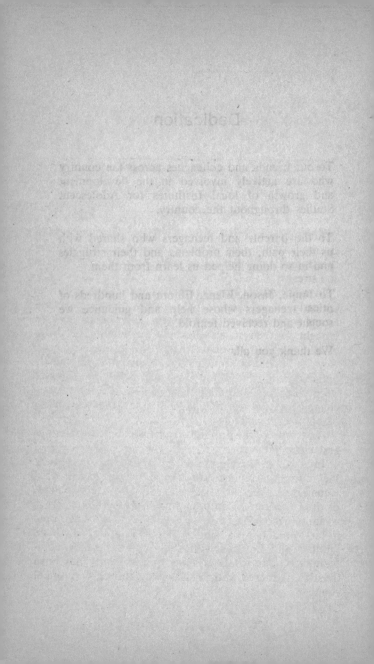

Introduction

Never before has it been harder to be a teenager. It's harder still today to be the parents of a teenager.

Adolescence has always been difficult, but today in our fast-changing industrial society, being a teenager is greatly complicated by the additional choices and stresses placed on a teenager.

In addition to the normal trauma of adolescence, the early sixties brought with them a change in sexual norms and mores in this country. The late sixties also brought an almost unbelievable availability of drugs of all types into the mainstream of adolescent society. Now, in addition to what is normally an extremely difficult time of life for the teen, two more stresses were placed on the adolescent in the late seventies—changing sexual norms and mores and the availability of both legal and illegal drugs.

And what of the parents of teenagers in the seventies and eighties?

In addition to trying to parent an adolescent through the normal turbulence of adolescence, a parent of a teenager was now forced to deal with the problems of drugs and sex. Compounding these problems, there is an enormous increase of divorce and we have seen a large number of single parent families, divorced families and families with step-parents become commonplace. Our whole concept of the family has been drastically altered and is still going through continual changes.

Some of the things you won't find in this book, although they may be touched on throughout the text, are the philosophy of adolescence, the growth and developmental stages of adolescence, and religion and the adolescent. All of these subjects have been well documented in other books.

This book is intended be a set of guidelines for those parents who are looking for a how-to book that will tell them specifically and in detail what they can do to help their teen make it to adulthood.

We have diligently tried to keep a balance between male and female examples throughout this book. We wish also to note that in the interest of flow and clarity, we have used the pronoun "he" and the possessive pronoun "his" rather than "he/she," "him/her" or "s/he."

CHAPTER 1

Purpose of this Book

The purpose of this book is to help you live with your teenager as amicably and as harmoniously as possible.

SURVIVOR'S HANDBOOK

Some of you may use this book as a survivor's handbook. Others may use it as a roadmap pinpointing a way through the hairy, mined jungle of your youngster's teenage years. It is our hope that you will find in this book the support and help you need as you travel with your teen on his way to adulthood. This is a how-to book that gives you specific methods and ideas to help you as a parent cope with and enjoy this exciting, emotionally draining, and mixed-up time of life for your teenager. Included in the book are hints on how you can help your teen, not only to "make it" through this no-man's land, but to enjoy those exciting pre-adult years.

If all you get from this book is an awareness that it is a near-impossible task to raise a teenager today, and that you are not the only parent who is having difficulties, then we have accomplished at least part of our goal in writing this book.

We have found that parents are looking for a book that spotlights teenagers; one that will tell them how

1

to recognize problems; one that will alert them to danger signals; one that will show them when and how to seek help. And they are looking for a book that will help them communicate with that adorable baby who overnight has grown up into a hard-to-handle, touchy, sometimes silent, sometimes seething, sometimes hard-to-love teenager.

The emphasis of this book will be on how to help you be a better parent and how to help you live with your teenager in an easier, more fulfilling, satisfying way. We will consider ourselves successful, if, after you have read the book, you can say that you understand what we've said and that you're willing to put these skills to work in your family.

Being a good parent is a highly complex and complicated skill and until recently, there were few places one could go to learn the skill of parenting.

We become parents and take on the awesome responsibility of loving and caring for a child from birth to adulthood without receiving any training or acquiring any special skills! We certainly wouldn't go to a doctor who wasn't trained, or a dentist, or a therapist. Yet, we seldom give thought to the fact that we have acquired very few, if any, skills in how to parent.

Most of us parent as we were parented. Since our own experience as children and teenagers comes from our parents, in raising our children we often use the same methods our parents used when they were raising us. The problem is that many of our parents were not very good at what they did—neither were our grandparents or our great-grandparents. Most of them tried hard to do things they felt were "right" and "good for us," but they had few opportunities to learn what was "right" or "good." It is only during the last decade that very many parenting classes have been offered by schools, colleges, church groups and women's clubs. But even today these classes reach only a small percentage of the parent population.

Parents today parent as well as they can. If you had fairly effective parents, the job of raising your children may be a bit easier, but it would certainly be a more gratifying experience if you had some specific parenting skills. For those of you who had unhappy childhood years and unhappy teenage years, it becomes an almost awesome task and formidable challenge to raise your children—for you, parenting skills are even more important.

The teens we see in therapy and communication classes say that their parents don't give them what they need; their parents are too critical of them and put them down frequently, their parents don't spend any time with them, their parents rarely talk to them, their parents don't give them a chance.

We find it very common for parents to do to their children what their parents did to them. A father who never spends any time with his teen probably did not have much time spent with him by his father when he was a teen. A mother who rarely talks to her teen except to tell her what to do and what not to do probably did not have any sharing time between her (when she was a teen) and her mother. Since our primary role model for parenting our children is our parents—most of whom didn't have the opportunity to learn parenting skills—how can we hope to do a good job when all we've got going for us is a poor role model and no skills?

This book will teach you specific skills which will help you to be a more effective parent. Parenting can be learned just like any other skill. If you're an excellent cook, you probably didn't start out that way. You went through a period of trial and error and most likely many meals were barely edible in the beginning. If you're a good gardener, you had to learn about soil and plants from someone who had this skill or you had to study books and articles until you learned the basic skills of gardening.

If you're a good tennis player, you had lessons and/or countless hours of practice before you could call yourself a competent player. Then what about parenting? Why is it that we expect people to become instantly wisdom-filled, skilled parents simply because a child has been born into a family? Parenting is something we have to learn.

Dr. Thomas Gordon, the author of *Parent Effectiveness Training,* and Dr. Fitzhugh Dodson, the author of *How to Parent,* to name just two people who are considered experts in their fields, realize the necessity of giving parents some workable parenting skills. Our book specifically focuses on parenting skills for teenagers—skills that enable parents not only to cope with their children and to lead happier lives, but skills that enable them to be more effective parents. Where else but at home do children learn parenting skills? Just the fact that you've bought this book and have read this far, tells us that you want to be a better parent, and more importantly, that you're willing to consider making some changes to achieve your goal.

Openness To Try Something New

Most people find it hard to change. There are many reasons for this. Psychotherapists agree that change is not easy.

It's not easy for any member of the family, whether teen or adult, to change. If you as a parent were happy about the way things are going in your life and in the life of your teenager, you probably wouldn't be reading this book. The fact that you are means that you're looking for a new way. But this new way is going to require some change on your part and change is difficult.

Every year people make New Year's resolutions and most of them are doomed to failure. People who make resolutions certainly do mean to keep them, but in order to keep them some change is needed on the part of the person making the resolutions.

Bookstore owners tell us that January is the biggest month for sales of how-to books. January is the month of new resolutions and people find that alone they can't follow through on their good intentions—maybe with the help of a how-to book they feel they can. We don't know what month you bought this book, but we can assume that you bought it because you want to make some changes. You want to know how to add to your repertoire of skills in parenting. But, we want to give you a warning. Making changes and putting into practice the ideas and methods in this book will be hard work. As we mentioned before, it will be hard for you to change and it's going to be hard for your teenager to change. Most parents realize that if they want things to go better in their families, they, the parents, will have to make some changes. When parents change, teenagers respond to those changes and conflicts decline.

Working at changing will not be easy; it's going to require some effort on your part. It might be helpful to think of change as you think of a job: both require work, an output of energy. There will be some trial and error—and that's okay, that's how we learn.

How Change Takes Place

Change is usually a two-step process. First, we gain some insight and awareness about a behavior—something that we're doing or not doing. That's the first step. The second step is when we start to incorporate those insights and awarenesses into changing that behavior. Both steps must take place before change can occur.

We are always most blind and least objective about ourselves. This book will help you increase your awareness and insight into your present behavior. But remember, that's only the first step in the two-step process of change. A lot of people who have insight and awareness about their behavior are not able to incorporate that insight and awareness into a behavior change. For example, someone may be aware that he drinks too much, yet is not able to stop that behavior. An overweight person may be aware that he overeats, and in some instances, even why; yet he is not able to stop that behavior. So, before change can come about, a person, in addition to being aware, must take that second and most important step and incorporate that awareness into some behavior change. This book will help you gain the awareness and the insight that you need and then will help you incorporate that awareness and insight into your behavior so that a change can take place.

Keeping a Journal

> *One of the most effective ways to help people become aware of the things they do and to incorporate that awareness into the desired behavior change is by keeping a journal.*

Remember, we never said that change was going to be easy, and this book's first assignment is going to be hard. But, keeping a journal is very important and it is a key part of this book's philosophy, which is to help you live with your teenager amicably and harmoniously. If both parents keep journals, obviously, it will be more effective than if only one parent does. This journal can be a simple, inexpensive notebook purchased from a stationery store—it doesn't have to be an elaborate hardback book.

You'll find it easier to keep a journal if you can

set aside the same time each day to write in it. Maybe the best time for you is as soon as you get up in the morning and you can write in it while you're having your first cup of coffee. Or maybe your day is scheduled differently and it may be more convenient for you to write in the evening. Anything that works for you is fine. The only thing we ask you to do is to put aside some time each day and make sure that time is the same time each day for your journal entries.

Each Journal Exercise should be completed at your own speed. For some parents, an exercise may be completed in one sitting, for others, it may take several days. We find that parents who take the time they need and don't rush, gain a better understanding and thus find it easier to implement the skills. Some exercises will go faster for you than others. If at all possible, each exercise should be completed before going on. If you find that some exercises are more difficult for you than others, do the best you can and continue on.

QUESTIONS ABOUT THE JOURNAL

Here are some commonly asked questions about the Journal.

How long should each exercise take?

There is no specified time for each exercise. Take all the time you need to complete each assignment. The important thing is to try not to skip or leave out any exercise.

What goes in the Journal?

In your Journal write out the exercise and then the answer to each exercise. Remember, there are no "wrong" answers. The Journal is a tool for you to use to help you become aware of your behaviors—those behaviors you want to keep and/or expand upon, and those behaviors you no longer want.

Do I complete an exercise before I go on?

Yes, if at all possible, complete an exercise before going on to the next chapter. You can always go back and add to your Journal if you find that you forgot to list something.

How do I know if I've done it right?

When you have answered each question completely and have followed any other directions given in a specific Journal Exercise, you have done it right.

When do I do each Journal Exercise?

Each Journal Exercise should be completed as you come to it. Completing the exercises will reinforce the skill learned in that chapter.

After I learn one communication skill do I practice it until I do it well before I go on to the next skill?

You may choose to do this if you want, or you may continue on to the next skill. You are the judge—you alone determine when to move on to the next skill.

Will the book help me if I don't do the exercises?

The exercises are a way of helping you practice your skills. A few parents may be able to read the book and immediately put the skills to work. Others will need the Journal Exercises and the practice they give before they feel comfortable using the skills.

Where can I learn more about these skills?

There is (or will be soon) a local Institute for Adolescent Studies where you can attend a six-week course called, *How To Live With Your Teenager*. This twelve-hour course meets one night a week, for six weeks, two hours each session. Chapter 16 will give you more information on local Institutes.

We don't expect any of you to be very enthusiastic or overjoyed with this assignment. At least in the beginning, people look upon it as a chore, and it is. It is one more thing to do in a parent's busy, busy day. It may even be boring in the beginning and certainly it will take a little time. But remember what we said earlier—changing is hard work. If you're really committed to changing the climate or tone in your household, keeping a journal is the most effective way we know to start.

CHAPTER 2

What You Need to Know
About Your Teenager

Before learning some skills on how to live with
and help your teen, you need to know some things
about him. This is not going to be a textbook explanation of the psychological development of adolescence,
but rather highlights of some key psychological "facts"
of adolescence.

*Part of what you need to know about your teen-
ager is what we call age-appropriate behavior.
Age-appropriate behavior means those behaviors
that are normal, natural and appropriate for an
adolescent. These same behaviors may not be
age-appropriate for a child or a young adult.*

Many parents do not know what these age-appropriate behaviors are for an adolescent. Some parents
are not aware that there are great differences between
age-appropriate behaviors for a teen and age-appropriate behaviors for a child. The differences are quite
surprising and sometimes shocking to parents.

NOT CONFIDING

*One facet of adolescence which seems to shock
parents is that their teen, who as a child, confided in them all the time, now rarely wants to
talk to them at all—about anything. This is age-
appropriate behavior for the adolescent.*

Very often the adolescent doesn't know how he feels. He is experiencing feelings that are totally new to him, and he can't even begin to put these feelings into words. He feels embarrassed and confused because he can't express these feelings. He doesn't understand them and doesn't want to admit that to his parents, so he no longer confides or shares things with them.

The teen also has many thoughts and opinions that he knows (the reality factor here is strong) his parents will not agree with. These thoughts and opinions may fall within the areas of drugs, sex, racial biases, religion, etc.

Parents sometimes react very strongly when their teens do not confide in them, and believe they have failed as parents. They feel upset because they don't know why their youngster stopped confiding in them. Parents of teens need to realize that not confiding in them, not talking over their problems with them, not discussing their feelings and ideas with them, is age-appropriate behavior.

Allowing your teen the space he needs to be himself, not pushing him, and yet at the same time letting him know that you're there when he needs you: this is the delicate balancing act parents of teens need to perfect.

Mood Swings

Drastic, lightning-quick changes of feelings and moods are totally age-appropriate for the adolescent. This is normal and natural teen behavior and while parents find it irritating, exasperating and difficult to live with, it may help to realize that "this, too, shall pass."

*Teenagers sulk, get angry, are crabby, are irra-
tional, are furious, are seething, are loving, are
generous, are warm, are giving, are tolerant, are
understanding. All these feelings (and others)
switch back and forth very quickly for a teenager.*

A TEEN'S NEED NOT TO BE WITH HIS FAMILY

When a child becomes a teenager he needs time to
be alone, time to be and talk with his friends, and
time to participate in outside activities. All of this
time adds up to time away from his family. He needs
to become a person separate from his family, to begin
to discover who he is and who he wants to be as a
person. This process of separating spans several years
and is a necessary, normal, and natural part of the
teenager's development. In terms of behavior, he may
not want to spend very much, if any, time with his
family. He may refuse to go with the family when
the family goes out; he may not want to spend holidays with his family; he may not even want to eat with
his family very often. He simply wants to separate—
to have time away from his family.

Parents have a difficult time accepting this kind of
behavior. Suddenly, their delightful youngster, who
wanted to spend a lot of time with them, who was
nice to have around, who was a joy to relate to—
now has become a moody, surly, rebellious teenager
who seems to reject them and resists being with them.
When this happens, parents frequently take this rejec-
tion personally and they demand that their teen spend
more time with them. Fights start over this issue,
communication stops and everyone is unhappy.

When a youngster becomes a teen, his need to
spend time with his family may decline at an accelerated rate. As a parent of a teenager, when this

happens, try to understand and accept his need to be away from you.

A teenager is not a child, he is an adolescent. A teenager doesn't need his parents in the same way he did when he was a child. This is one of the greatest challenges parents of teenagers have to face—their teens need them differently now, and parents have to respond to that difference.

Invite your teen to go out with the family to dinner or to a movie. Invite him to be a part of all family outings. The teen needs to know that he is welcome to join in all family activities. On the other hand, the parents need to understand and accept the fact that their teen needs to be alone and away from them at times and very often will not join family activities.

One word of caution here: as a parent, you need to work very hard NOT to make your teen feel guilty about his need to be alone and away from you. Otherwise, your teen will feel that it's not all right to accept all his feelings.

Need To Rebel

A teenager needs to rebel or to reject, or to try on different ideas and values. It is the teenager's way of defining himself.

It is a natural and normal part of adolescence for the adolescent to rebel against the values and beliefs of his parents and of society.

This means he is trying to define his own values and beliefs separate from yours. He may conclude this process by thinking and believing similarly or dissimilarly from you. The point is that the values and beliefs will feel more "his" to him if he can complete this process.

Think back to when you were a teenager. Did you hold the same values as your parents? Were you in perfect agreement with your parents? Probably not. Did you lie? Did you cheat? Did you steal? Did you do things "behind your parents' backs"? Probably yes!

The teenager who is a "goody-goody" (and not many of them truly are) is one who always listens to his parents and never gets into trouble, in other words, the "perfect" kid. The "perfect" kid doesn't rebel at all—and almost always that "perfect" teen will experience problems as an adult because he did not meet that mandatory growth requirement during adolescence, which is to REBEL—to try on different values and beliefs, to define himself. The truly "perfect" teen should be seen by a therapist in order to help him avoid psychological problems—sometimes severe psychological problems—as an adult.

There are many non-harmful ways for a teen to rebel or define himself, such as choice of music, sound level of music, hair style, messy room, sleeping late, clothes, jewelry, beliefs, etc. And, while it is not necessary for parents to like any of the non-harmful ways their teens choose to rebel, it is imperative to remember that the teen is fulfilling a psychological need when he does rebel.

Before you do battle over your teen's long hair and loud music, make sure he has other non-harmful ways of rebelling. Otherwise, you may win the battle but lose the war when he chooses to rebel in a way you find totally unacceptable.

PEER GROUP PRESSURE

Another psychological need that is crucial to the adolescent is his need for peer group acceptance.

As the adolescent rebels against society and parental values, he seeks acceptance and support from his peer group. The less acceptance and support that the teen gets at home, either from parents or older family members, the more he will seek from his peer group. However, no matter how much acceptance and support he gets at home, he will still seek acceptance and approval from his peer group.

During adolescence, the peer group influence is at its greatest, and often, if the adolescent is forced to make a choice, he will choose the peer group's values rather than parental values.

Dr. Fred Streit, in his booklet, entitled, *Parents and Problems: Through the Eyes of Youth,* developed a picture graph of the estimated periods of influence which three major factors have on a child and a rough indication of the strength of that influence.

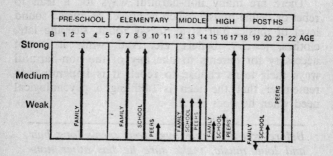

As you can see, the peer influence or pressure far outweighs all others in high school and afterwards. In junior high, peer pressure is equally as strong as family and school.

These are the key psychological "facts" of adolescence. The background and skills you need to help you survive your youngster's teen years start in the next chapter.

There is something very special about the teen years. With parenting skills at your fingertips, your child's adolescent years can be an enriching and gratifying experience for you both.

CHAPTER 3

Self-Esteem

Self-esteem means a feeling of regard, respect and affection for one's self.

Just going through the adolescence growth period almost always produces a self-esteem problem for the teen. There are very, very few adolescents who do not have self-esteem problems. Most teens don't like certain aspects of themselves, and generally may have a lowered and variable and undefined opinion of themselves, and their looks, and have a variable self-esteem quotient, although some of their behavior may be geared toward covering up this lack.

Now what happens? A teen with generally lowered and variable self-esteem problems, needing to meet the psychological need to rebel, to challenge parental authority and values, and to define himself, has set the stage for CONFLICT. Not one CONFLICT, but CONFLICT after CONFLICT after CONFLICT after CONFLICT. And what are the results? Emotionally battered parents and teenagers. Self-esteem is constantly gained and lost during these conflicts—both by parents and by teenagers. Parents many times feel less and less able to cope, they feel that they are losing hold and that things are getting beyond their control. They try this and that; they withdraw or lash out. The situation, however, doesn't change. It's still there in pulsating, living color!

The teens lose, too. They feel less sure of their parents' love. Their need for acceptance and approval gets greater and greater because they're getting less and less of it at home. They have rebelled (as they must) and as a result, they lost so much in the rebellion that their self-esteem and their self-image are at a much lowered and unstable point. The adolescent who has lost approval from his parents now has a void in his life. Granted many times that void was created by his rebellion, which is a necessary part of this growth period, but this void is not being filled at home by parents and older family members. There is only one place left for the teen to fill this void—he seeks the approval and acceptance of his peer group more and more.

Another great challenge to parents: to give praise and support to their teens who, embroiled in the dynamics of adolescence, are starving for praise and support from their parents.

This *does not* mean that you praise and support every difference encountered as right and good. It *does* mean that you support and praise, where possible. In other words, trust your teen's need to be different and his ability to choose and make up *his* mind—right or wrong, with good and not-so-good consequences.

It's going to take a conscious effort on your part as a parent to give your teen the praise and support he needs.

How many times have you come down hard on your teen? How many times have you been genuinely supportive? Did you take the time to talk to your teenager? Did you refuse to talk when your teenager wanted to? Did you speak to each other today at all? When was the last time you just listened, listened without giving advice or making judgmental statements? When was the last time you did something special for your teenager?

If you feel that you've failed this quiz, hold on,

help's coming. You have already taken the first step in the change process: you have gained some insight and awareness of your past behavior. You are reading this book which indicates that you are seeking alternatives. Step one is well underway. Now comes step two: incorporating those insights and that awareness into your present behavior.

Maintenance Talk

Frequently, parents of teenagers find that most of the talk between them and the teen is maintenance talk, such as, "Did you take the garbage out?," "Pick up your room," "Put the cat out," etc. The responses parents generally get from their teen might be: "Later," "Yeah," "Get off my back!," etc. There isn't a genuine caring interaction in any of the three statements or responses above. A household cannot survive without a certain amount of maintenance talk, but it needs to be surrounded with many caring statements and responses.

Who makes the first attempt? Who takes the first step? You, as parents, have that responsibility. If YOU don't start, it won't happen.

But first, let's talk about *your* self-esteem. Because of the pressures and stresses unique to our day and age, raising an adolescent is a nearly impossible task! When a parent encounters difficulties in trying to carry out this task, the parent's self-esteem drops and he starts to doubt his effectiveness as a parent and sometimes as a spouse and a person.

The parents we talk to often feel that they've done a terrible job of raising their teen. They consider themselves failures as parents. They think they're totally incompetent. They feel guilty—sometimes they are overwhelmed with guilt—they don't know what to do. All they do know is that whatever they've been doing is wrong. Frequently, because of a particular problem or crisis, these parents feel they are "going through hell."

A TYPICAL PARENT

If your teen is having problems with drugs, problems at school, problems with friends, etc., you're not unusual—in fact you're probably a typical parent.

Don't torture yourself about the things you did in the past that you feel may be the reasons for your teen's problems today. What happened before is past. You can't change the past—what you can change is today and tomorrow. You can make life better for you, for your teen and for your entire family by becoming a more effective parent. The skills you'll be learning will enhance you as a person and as a parent. They will do the same for your teen.

Earlier we mentioned that the best way to become aware of what we are doing or not doing is to keep a journal. If you take the time to think something through and to write it down, it will help you see your life as it is and it will help you to plan the changes you want to make.

An inexpensive notebook and a pencil are all you need. Allow a page or two (or more) for each Journal Exercise. Again, we suggest that you put aside a special time each day—preferably the same time each day—to do your Journal Exercises.

Journal Exercise #1 is about you. Its objective is to help you feel good about yourself and the job you are doing as a parent.

JOURNAL EXERCISE #1

Write down everything you like about yourself as a parent. Be specific. List as many attributes as you can. If you can't think of any attributes that you have today, go back a few years or so.

For example, some entries might be:

1. I go to most of my son's basketball games.
2. I watched a television program with my teen a few days ago.
3. I spend time listening to my daughter tell me about school.
4. I didn't yell about his hair today.
5. I baked cookies for my daughter's home room bake sale.

If you're still having trouble thinking of some good attributes, give yourself a little time. Sometimes it's very hard to think of ourselves in positive ways. We can frequently get into a rut of negativism, and if someone asks us what we think is wrong with us, we probably could list ten or twenty things in less than five minutes! We want you to list only those things you think are *good* about you. If you need help, ask a friend you trust.

As you're doing the other Journal Exercises, and you think of something good about you, list it—keep adding to this list. It can be as long as you want it to be.

The next several chapters will teach you communication skills—parenting skills. Similar communication skills are taught in some businesses to middle and upper management. They work!

Take your time. Reread those sections which are not clear to you. When you think you have learned a skill, practice it first outside your home. Try it with friends, neighbors, people at work. When you're feeling confident about the process, try it at home.

If you falter and it doesn't work for you right away, hang in there, try it again—IT WILL WORK!

CHAPTER 4

Listening

Knowing how to listen is probably the most important communication tool there is. So few parents listen well. To listen we must be attentive. We must be still, and yet encourage thought in others. Our full attention must be directed to the person who is speaking.

If parents learned and used only the listening skill, it would cut down many of the conflicts in the home. It is such an easy skill to learn, but a difficult one to use or put into practice.

Two criteria are necessary for listening effectively:

1. As the listener, you must be accepting of the individual. This does not mean that you must accept the situation, only the person. (For example, your teen brings home a report card with two F's on it. In order to be a good listener, you don't need to accept the F's on the report card—you need only accept your teen. In other words, you need to separate the action or behavior from the person.)

2. As the listener, you must take the time and the interest to listen.

If these two criteria are met, you are ready to begin the process of listening. Before we can begin this process, we need to be able to read other people's body language, as well as be aware of our own body language.

Dr. Noel Burch, co-author (with Dr. Thomas Gordon) of *Teacher Effectiveness Training,* using Dr. Ray L. Birdwhistell's research (University of Pennsylvania), says that when a person is communicating, 70% of his message is sent by his body language, 23% by the tone or inflection of his voice and only 7% by the words he uses.

We need to hear more than the words. We need to hear the feeling or mood behind the words. To put it another way we need to hear first the "music" and then listen to the words or "lyrics." When someone is singing, the feeling or mood is expressed by the music and then reinforced with the words or lyrics. To hear and translate this "music" we need to be able to read the other person's body language as well as to be aware of our own body language.

Body language is a non-verbal form of communication. Many books have been written on the subject and some study the subject in great depth. It's not necessary to be an expert on body language before you can consider yourself a good listener. The things you need to know about body language are few. First of all, you need to be aware of your own body language.

YOUR BODY LANGUAGE

As a listener, your body language must communicate in a non-verbal way that you are accepting, that you are non-judgmental, that you are non-evaluating. Remember your body language acts out what you are feeling.

If you are relaxed, have a pleasant, open expression on your face and you have eye contact, your body language is sending a message of acceptance, non-judgment and non-evaluation.

Body language that is inappropriate for a listener would be:

1. Turning your back to the person who is speaking.
2. Drumming your fingers on a table or chair while a person is speaking to you.
3. Not maintaining eye contact with the person who is speaking.
4. Yawning while a person is speaking to you.
5. Rummaging through a drawer or a cupboard—or otherwise moving around while a person is speaking to you.
6. Checking your wristwatch or a clock while a person is speaking to you.
7. Carrying on another conversation while a person is speaking to you.

ETC., ETC., ETC.

The list could go on and on.

For example, if your teenager, George, comes home and says to you:

GEORGE: "Mom, something happened at school today."

And you reply with a great deal of exasperation, your back to him and your head in a cupboard noisily looking for a pan:

MOM: "Okay, what happened now?"

The chances of your finding out what happened at school have just dropped to -10! The reason being that your body language is sending a much stronger message than your words. Your body language is saying, "I really don't care what happened at school today. Can't you see I'm too busy to talk to you now!"

When you use appropriate body language, you send a message that says: "I want to listen—you're important to me." With that kind of message, your teen will be much more willing to talk to you.

The following Journal Exercise will help you become more aware of your own body language.

JOURNAL EXERCISE #2

List five messages someone in your family sent you this week. Beside each message write what your body language was when you were listening. Was it appropriate or inappropriate? For example:

Message sent to me *   *My Body Language*
Tim wanted me to go   No eye contact. I was
see him play soccer on   busy doing dishes so my
Friday.   back was to him.

_____Appropriate **X** Inappropriate

My wife told me that   No eye contact, I was
things weren't going   reading the paper. One
well at her office.   of the younger children
                             was yelling and I went
                             to check on him.

_____Appropriate **X** Inappropriate

* If you can't remember, do this exercise tomorrow and make a special effort to remember and be aware of your body language.

Our body language sends a message that speaks louder than all our words.

THE OTHER PERSON'S BODY LANGUAGE

The other person's—or the speaker's—body language is a clue to us. It helps us tune into his mood or his feelings. Here again, we need only know the very obvious body language messages. For example:

Body Language   *Possible Feelings*
Tears   Joy, happiness, hurt,
                         sorrow, frustration

Slamming things	Anger, frustration, feeling helpless
Smile	Happy, self-satisfaction
Yawn	Tired, bored
Rigid body stance	Unsure, scared, frightened

Here again, we could go on and on with our list. Let's take the same example. Your teenager, George, comes home and says to you:

GEORGE: (eyes downcast, body slouched forward, with a catch in his voice says): "Mom, something happened at school today."

His words, "Mom, something happened at school today," don't convey anywhere near the real message. But his body language may be saying: "Something's wrong; things aren't going right; I'm scared and upset." Now, you've got a much more complete message.

The following Journal Exercise will give you practice in reading other people's body language.

JOURNAL EXERCISE #3

Speak to five different people and write in your journal the person's name, their body language and your translation of that body language. For example:

Person spoken to: *Body Language* *Translation*

| Joe | No eye contact —he was looking at the floor. | nervous, didn't seem to want to talk to me. |
| | Had his hands in his pockets. | uncomfortable |

	Had a pained expression on his face.	upset
Joan	Eye contact.	interested
	Smile on her face	happy
	Relaxed body stance.	confident

Why do we need to be able to read a person's body language and his voice tone? Why does Dr. Burch say that our words are only 7% of our message?

Frequently, the words we say are not enough—they may be coded. A teen especially may send a coded message. We send coded messages because we're not sure it's "all right" to have or express certain feelings.

The only totally honest people in this world are tiny tots! That's right. They are the only ones who say exactly what they want, mean exactly what they say, and say it when they want to say it. Then "society" makes them conform. We say to them, "Don't say that in public," "Don't scratch there," "That's not nice to do," "Don't trust anybody," "People don't like people who do that," "Girls don't do that," "Boys don't do that," and so on. This could be another one of those endless lists!

We all have to conform—the world would be a wild place if everyone did what they wanted when they wanted. But by conforming, we pay a price. And that price is we don't always say what we mean because we're not sure how our message is going to be received. Sometimes there is only one thing left to do, we code our messages. We send only a little of it at a time. If we find that the other person accepts and understands what we're trying to say, we say more. Eventually, in a mutually trusting relationship, more messages are uncoded than are coded. However, it takes a while to get there.

By recognizing that a person sends his message in three parts: body language, tone of voice, and words, we have a better chance of translating the true message.

In addition to being able to read the speaker's non-verbal message, we need to enlarge our vocabulary of "feeling" words. We need to be able to name the message. We sometimes get into a rut when it comes to descriptive word usage and may use only five words to express a whole gamut of feelings. These five words are: nice, mad, glad, sad and angry. These are good words, but there are many more feeling words we could use that might more accurately describe a feeling. For instance, we may use "glad" to cover a lot of happy feelings, but how about using instead, such words as: elated, thrilled, ecstatic, excited, euphoric—if they fit the situation, why not use them?

The next Journal Exercise is really a vocabulary exercise. The object is to see if you can think of twenty positive feeling words and twenty negative feeling words. Having these words in your vocabulary will be a great help to you as you learn your new listening skill.

JOURNAL EXERCISE #4

In your Journal list 20 positive feeling words (such as: happy, gratified, satisfied, thrilled, etc.) and 20 negative feeling words (such as: sad, dejected, depressed, unhappy, etc.).

Keep this list handy because you will be using these words in formulating your listening responses in the next Journal Exercise.

To be an effective listener, you need to know how to listen attentively—with your whole being. We call this listening skill ATTENTIVE LISTENING.

ATTENTIVE LISTENING (A-L)

The attentive listening skill is used when someone we care about wants to talk.

The person doing the speaking may be angry or frustrated or bursting with joy. He may have a problem he needs to talk about and perhaps find a solution for, he may just need to air out or ventilate some feelings of anger, or he may need to "spread a little sunshine" and share with you a joyful happening in his life. Whatever his reasons for talking, your skill is the same.

We must gear ourselves to *listen* and *not react* to what's being said. Some parents find this hard to do, even though the concept is quite simple.

Listening in and of itself is a passive activity. Some parents disapprove of any passive or non-directive activity especially when it comes to teenagers. And, granted, the word "passive" is linked in our minds with "weak" or "uncertain," etc. So, their approach is to over-react to the other person's message and attempt to control the conversation, which totally defeats the goal of listening.

Following is an example of an exchange between 15-year-old John and his mother. John has just come home from school.

JOHN: (comes in the front door, slams it shut, throws his books on the dining room table, and says in a very agitated voice) "I don't care if that damn place burns down. For all I care, the whole damn place can go to hell and . . ."

MOM: (interrupting, says through clenched teeth):

"How many times do I have to tell you I don't like that kind of language? If you want me to listen to what you have to say, keep it clean. (Pause) Well, I'm waiting."

JOHN: (turns his back to his mother and shouts): "You don't want to hear about it—you'd be on their side anyhow." (Walks out of the room, into his bedroom and slams the door again.)

MOM: (Shaking her head and mumbling to herself): "What did I do to deserve such a kid. (louder) You stay in your room until your father comes home and we'll talk about your language later!"

John has indicated both verbally—with his words and tone of voice—and non-verbally—by his body language—that he wants to talk, that he wants someone to listen to him. His non-verbal message is sent by his body language: slamming the door, throwing his books on the table. His tone of voice sends an even clearer message. The message: "Something happened, things are not right with me, I may talk if someone will listen to me."

Now, in addition to the above message, John has also sent a verbal message—but unfortunately for John, he couched it in language that his mother finds offensive. John's mother hears only his words. She misses completely the greater part of his message—body language and his tone of voice. She heard his words and then reacted to those words and immediately attempted to control the conversation. The outcome is that neither John nor his mother is happy with the interaction, and more importantly, John now has two problems: whatever happened before he came home and now his mother's reaction.

We use the ATTENTIVE LISTENING skill to tune into the feeling behind the word message. We will not always be able to rely on the words in a message. Dr. Burch's communication breakdown told us that the words are only 7% of our message. If we want to get more of the message, we are going to have to find it by reading the body language. A person's body language and tone of voice will give us the feeling or mood of a message. Again, using Dr. Burch's breakdown, if we correctly read the body language message we have 70% of the message. If we correctly hear the feeling or mood of the tone of voice, we have an additional 23% of the message.

Now we have to indicate by our reply to the speaker that we have heard what he is trying to say. At the beginning we strongly suggest that you use the following somewhat structured reply formula until searching out the feeling or mood behind a person's words becomes second nature to you.

Use the phrase, *"You're feeling (add here whatever feeling word is appropriate)."* If you chose an on-target feeling word or phrase the speaker will send you another message (this time less coded) and again, you reply, *"You're feeling (choose another feeling word or phrase which you feel is appropriate)."*

Try to choose the correct feeling word. If you miss the correct word, the person who is speaking will tell you that's not what he's feeling, and then you try again.

Let's take John's problem again. This time his father will use his ATTENTIVE LISTENING skill:

JOHN: (comes in the front door, slams it shut, throws his books on the dining room table, and in an agitated voice says): "I don't care if that damn place burns down. For all I care, the whole damn place can go to hell and . . . oh, what's the use!"

DAD: (very concerned)
"Boy, *you're* really *feeling upset!"* (A-L)

JOHN: (angrily)
"You would be, too, Dad! That coach doesn't know a damn thing about coaching!"

DAD: (still very concerned)
      "You're feeling really down—like you've lost
      something." (A-L)

JOHN: (less agitated, less angry)
      "It just wasn't fair, Dad, I've made all the
      practices and the coach had just about promised
      me a spot on the starting team. Then this new
      guy, Joe, comes out for his first practice and
      comes on real good and the coach says, 'That's
      the kind of talent I want on the first string
      team.' "

DAD: (with lots of care and concern)
      "You're feeling unappreciated and it's hard to
      understand something like that." (A-L)

JOHN: (more relaxed now)
      "Yeah. Some guys just have the knack, I guess.
      With me it takes practice, practice and more
      practice. (Pause) But, I'll say one thing for
      that new kid, Dad, he's a natural."

DAD: (still caring and concerned)
      "You're feeling hurt though, just the same."
      (A-L)

JOHN: (feeling he's been heard, changes the subject):
      "Yeah. You're right, Dad. (brightening) Want
      to shoot a few baskets?"

John's father was truly listening to John. Dad was
hearing the music as well as the words. He didn't
react to John's angry language. What's more important, he encouraged John to air out or ventilate his
frustration and his disappointment. A parent who can
listen in this manner will frequently be pleasantly
surprised at the outcome.

The following Journal Exercise will give you some
practice in tuning into the feeling or mood behind the
words. It will also give you some practice in formulating ATTENTIVE LISTENING responses. Each problem below sets the stage for you by giving you the
body language, the tone of voice, and the word

statement. Using the ATTENTIVE LISTENING structured reply, write out a good ATTENTIVE LISTENING response for each situation.

JOURNAL EXERCISE #5

1. Body Language: chin on chest, shoulders slumped forward.
   Tone of Voice: low, catch in voice.
   Word Statement: "I'm never going home again."
   Write an ATTENTIVE LISTENING response in your Journal.

2. Body Language: clenched fists, rigid stance, teeth clenched, eyes blazing.
   Tone of Voice: pleading tone, loud voice.
   Word Statement: "Why do Mom and Dad fight so much?"

3. Body Language: face in her hands, crying.
   Tone of Voice: low, catch in voice.
   Word Statement: "I just can't tell my Mother, she'd kill me!"
   Write an ATTENTIVE LISTENING response in your Journal.

4. Body Language: arms in air, smile on her face.
   Tone of Voice: vibrant, loud.
   Word Statement: "I can't believe it—I got the part!"
   Write an ATTENTIVE LISTENING response in your Journal.

5. Body Language: eyes shining, smile on her face.
   Tone of Voice: medium tone, high pitch.
   Word Statement: "Joe finally asked me for a date!"

Write an ATTENTIVE LISTENING response in your Journal.

6. Body Language: shaking head, frown on forehead.
Tone of Voice: low tone, slowly spoken.
Word Statement: "Ellen wants me to take care of her pet snake while she's on vacation, Mom."
Write an ATTENTIVE LISTENING response in your Journal.

Now write in your Journal six real listening situations. Try out your new skill on your family, at work or at play. This exercise is completed when you have a total of twelve different listening responses.

Most of us can and want to solve our own problems—our teenagers included—if we're given an opportunity to search out solutions or alternatives in a supporting, trusting, caring way. Listening—ATTENTIVE LISTENING—does just that.

There are two goals of listening:
1. to help another air out, ventilate or share feelings,
2. to help another arrive at his own solutions or seek his own alternatives.

Whether you meet one or two of these goals depends solely on the *speaker*.

When the speaker stops talking, you stop listening. Don't force "endings" or solutions. The person who is speaking is "in charge" of the conversation—not the listener.

When you master the ATTENTIVE LISTENING skill, you will find lots of warm feelings are generated between the speaker and the listener. Where before there may have been antagonism, or sarcasm, now there is warmth and caring and concern.

CHAPTER 5

Straight Talk

When the other person has a problem or indicates in some way he's suffering discomfort, the skill to use is ATTENTIVE LISTENING.

If *you* have a problem or are experiencing discomfort, or you're angry, upset, irritated, etc., the skill to use is the STRAIGHT TALK skill and send an I-hurt message.

If you are happy about someone or something and you want to share that happiness with someone else, the skill to use is the STRAIGHT TALK skill and send an I-love or I-am-happy message. We'll be discussing the positive Straight Talk message skill in the next chapter when we talk about Praise.

I-HURT (NEGATIVE FEELING) MESSAGE

How can you take care of yourself without putting down or making judgments about another person, especially if that other person is the "problem"! Answer: by sending a simple message (with the appropriate body language) that tells how *you* feel about something, not a message that says what you think about the person who is causing you the problem. The two examples that follow point up the difference in each approach.

Incorrect

MOM: (with hands on her hips, says in a loud voice) "How many times do I have to tell you to

36

take out the garbage. If you weren't such a lazy, spoiled rotten kid, maybe I could get some work out of you!"

ELLEN: (in front of the T.V. with her book opened, mumbles) "I'm busy. I'm doing something important."

MOM: (louder) "What could be more important than getting this garbage emptied? Nothing! Act your age and do something around here!"

ELLEN: (not paying any attention) "Uh huh, later."

Here is the situation: The garbage needs to be emptied and Mom wants Ellen to do it. In her first statement, Mom is using sarcasm and name-calling. In her second statement, Mom has belittled and put down whatever activity is keeping Ellen from emptying the garbage. The goal is to get the garbage emptied—it has not been met and in the process both Mom and Ellen have lost some self-esteem. Mom believes she has lost some self-esteem because she has not been listened to and therefore in her eyes, not respected. Ellen has lost self-esteem because she has been called names, been put down and belittled—all in a sarcastic manner. And still the garbage is sitting in the kitchen!

Let's try another approach. The situation is still the same—Mom wants the garbage emptied.

Correct

MOM: (facing Ellen, says forcefully) "I feel angry and ignored when I say over and over again 'empty the garbage' because I feel like I'm the only one doing anything around here."

ELLEN: (looking up, a little concerned) "Okay, Mom, I'll do it just as soon as I finish my science project."

MOM: (warmly) "You'd like to finish one job before you start another."

ELLEN: (smiling, says excitedly) "This is something really special, Mom—want to see it? It's my project for science class and it's taken me forever to get this far. What do you think?"

MOM: (looking at the project, says proudly) "I really like it, Ellen. I bet that gets you an 'A'!"

ELLEN: (smiling, but a bit concerned) "Boy, I hope so, Mom. (pause) There, it's done."

MOM: (warmly, in a medium voice tone) "Great, Honey! How about the garbage now?"

ELLEN: (willingly) "You bet, Mom!"

Look at all the pluses in this last approach. Not only does the garbage get emptied, but Ellen feels good about herself, her science project and her Mom! Mom has really used ATTENTIVE LISTENING and feels closer and more loving toward Ellen in this last exchange than she did in the first exchange.

Let's take a closer look at Mom's first statement in the correct example above:

"I feel angry and ignored *when* I say over and over again 'empty the garbage' *because* I feel like I'm the only one doing anything around here."

The formula you need to know to send a Straight Talk message is: I feel *(whatever the feeling is)* when *(give a non-judgmental account of the situation—not the person and avoid using the pronoun "you")* because *(give a statement telling how it will affect you, the message-sender.)*

A simple concept, don't you agree? But, so difficult for parents to use. Let's take each part of a Straight Talk message separately: There are three parts: I feel, when, and because.

Part one: "I feel _____ . . ." It may be difficult for some parents to use the pronoun "I." It's a lot easier to talk about the other person—"you" this and "you" that—it's a lot safer, too. If I use "I" it means that I am revealing something about me—in this case, what I'm feeling. So, in a sense, I'm taking a bit of a risk. The older we get the harder it usually is for us to take risks, even an "I feel" risk. If you can master that step and get yourself to name yourself, you're halfway home! Now all you have to do to complete the first part of your Straight Talk message is to put a name to that feeling you're feeling. Remember, be descriptive in choosing your feeling words. Check your Journal Exercise #4 and the list of positive and negative feeling words in the back of the book. We're asking you to speak a different way, so we think it's only fair to give you some new or different vocabulary words to go with your new skills.

Taking a minute to choose a word that really describes what you're feeling helps you focus on you and your feeling. By focusing on your feeling, you are less apt to make a mistake in the second part of your message when you describe what's causing you the problem.

Let's look at some "I feel" statements—both right and wrong ones—about situations that are pretty common in households with teenagers.

Situation: Teens are snacking from the minute they come in from school and aren't hungry at dinnertime. They just pick at their food and then are ready to eat again soon after dinner. Parents don't think they are eating enough nutritious food.

"I feel" *Statement:* "I feel you kids are just ruining your health . . ." (WRONG: That feeling doesn't belong to the parent. It's a judgmental statement which may or may not be true.)

"I feel" *Statement:* "I feel frustrated (or I feel I am wasting money) . . ." (CORRECT: A parent might very possibly feel frustrated because of the work involved in preparing a meal —or, very possibly, especially with today's prices, a parent might think that money was being wasted when the food prepared was not being eaten.)

Situation: Teenage daughter's room is a sight. You really like a clean house and you have been after your daughter to clean her room for several days now.

"I feel"
Statement: "I feel angry and annoyed . . ." (CORRECT: Good start for the first part of this statement.)

"I feel"
Statement: "I feel you're not paying any attention to me . . ." (WRONG: This one probably won't work, because most parents have used it too many times before. In addition, it's not a true feeling statement, it's a judgment statement.)

Situation: Your son is a new driver. Dad has allowed him to drive the family car to a high school dance. He was to be home by midnight. It is now 2 a.m. and he has just pulled into the driveway.

"I feel"
Statement: "I feel you have no sense of responsibility . . ." (WRONG: That's not really what you're feeling; it's a judgment statement. Wouldn't "scared," "worried," or "upset" be more like it? Most likely you would be feeling all of these, but when you saw him pull into the driveway, your relief gave way to anger. Try to remember the feeling you had before anger took over. Chapter 11 discusses anger more fully.)

"I feel"
Statement: "I was beside myself with worry . . ." (CORRECT: Now, you've got your son's

attention. You haven't attacked him so he
won't be too defensive.)

The following Journal Exercise will give you some
practice in formulating the first part of a Straight Talk
negative message.

JOURNAL EXERCISE #6
  In your Journal write an "I feel _____"
statement for each of the following situations.
1. *Situation:* Jason comes to the dinner table
   with dirty hands and a dirty face.
2. *Situation:* Jill is playing the stereo exceedingly loud and you have a splitting headache.
3. *Situation:* Eddie and his friend George are
   playing catch in front of the house. One of
   them just missed—and the ball went through
   your living room window.
4. *Situation:* Joan has been on the phone for
   the last two hours talking to her girlfriends.
   You are expecting an important business
   call and you would like to keep the phone
   free.
5. *Situation:* Your friend whom you haven't
   seen for several months is visiting you with
   her three-year-old. The youngster is pulling
   leaves off your favorite plant.

Part two: ". . . when _____ . . ." Using
a "when" phrase, it is now necessary to describe in a
non-judgmental way what the situation is. Something
is happening or not happening that is causing you
some concern. The most difficult part of a Straight
Talk negative message is part two. We find it hard to
describe what's happening or not happening without
attaching blame to someone.

Your message can fail you if you mess up part two.

In the example about the garbage that needed to be emptied, Mom made it a point to note that fact several times. Mom said: "How many times do I have to tell *you,* to take out the garbage—if *you* weren't such a lazy, spoiled rotten kid, maybe I could get some work out of *you.*"

Mom resorted to sarcasm and name-calling. Her message puts down Ellen, evaluates her negatively and calls her names. Ellen's defensive reaction is to ignore the message: "I'm busy. I'm doing something important."

If Ellen's Mom took out the pronoun "you," she would also have to take out the sarcasm and the name-calling.

It's only natural *not* to want to do anything for someone who is calling you a rotten, lazy kid. So, remember, the focus of the "when" phrase must be on what's happening or not happening and it must be non-judgmental and free of blame. Here's a hint: avoid using the pronoun "you" in the "when" phrase. That will help you keep in mind that this phrase must be non-judgmental and free of blame.

When you do the second part of this message properly, there is a plus in it for you as a parent. While you are trying to describe the situation in a non-blameful way, you will be able to view your teen with less antagonism. Remember, you have already named your feeling—that alone will help you view the situation more calmly. Then you can see with a clearer eye what the situation really is. In other words, once you have tagged a name to your feeling, you can put it aside for a moment while you try to describe the situation in a non-blameful, non-judgmental way.

Let's take a look at some "when" phrases—both right and wrong ones—using the same situations.

Situation: Teens are snacking from the minute they come in from school and aren't hungry at dinnertime. They just pick at their food and then are ready to eat again soon after dinner. Parents don't think they are eating enough nutritious food.

"when"
Statement: ". . . when you binge on junk food and then don't eat dinner . . ."
(WRONG: We don't think that one will work because of the judgmental phrase: "*you* binge on junk food." The rest of the statement is a good one.)

"when"
Statement: ". . . when no one's hungry at dinnertime and dinner doesn't get eaten . . ."
(CORRECT: This one is a better "when" statement because it states some real concerns: no one is hungry enough to eat dinner and dinner doesn't get eaten.)

Situation: Teenage daughter's room is a sight. You really like a clean house and you've been after your daughter to clean her room for several days now.

"when"
Statement: ". . . when I say time after time 'clean your room' and nothing gets done . . ."
(CORRECT: That's a good "when" statement. It's almost impossible not to give ownership to the bedroom, so the possessive pronoun needs to be used here. However, its use is in no way judgmental and not to use it would sound too awkward.)

"when"
Statement: ". . . when my daughter doesn't listen to a thing I say . . ."
(WRONG: Probably won't work. Referring to your daughter in the third person is also too awkward. If you're like other parents, you've used the phrase, "doesn't listen to a thing I say," too many times in the past—whatever effectiveness it had is long since gone!)

Situation: Your son is a new driver. Dad has allowed him to drive the family car to a high school dance. He was to be home by midnight. It is now 2 a.m. and he has just pulled into the driveway.

"when"   ". . . when you broke your promise to me
Statement: and stayed out raising hell until 2 a.m. . . ."
(WRONG: Too many suppositions here, and you're not going to get the truth, if in fact, you get any answer at all.)

"when"   ". . . when 12:30 came and went and I
Statement: didn't hear from you . . ."
(CORRECT: This whole phrase is a statement of fact with no overtones of blame or judgment. The chances of your getting the whole, true story have increased one hundredfold.)

Let's put together what we have so far—a two-part Straight Talk negative message:

1. "I feel frustrated when no one's hungry at dinner-time and dinner doesn't get eaten."
2. "I feel angry and annoyed when I say time after time, 'clean your room,' and nothing gets done."
3. "I was beside myself with worry when 12:30 came and went and I didn't hear from you."

Each of the above messages could be sent as is— using only two parts instead of a three-part message. Two-part Straight Talk messages are perfectly good messages as they stand. The third part is optional.

If your body language and your tone of voice build on the feeling you're trying to express, these messages will do the job. No one suffers a loss of self-esteem. In fact, just the reverse is true—all parties increase their self-esteem because each will have an opportunity to be heard.

The following Journal Exercise will give you some

practice in formulating the "when" statement of a Straight Talk negative message.

JOURNAL EXERCISE #7

In your Journal write a two-part Straight Talk negative message. These situations are the same as you had in Journal Exercise #6. Use your "I feel" statement from this exercise and then add your "when" statement.

1. *Situation:* Jason comes to the dinner table with dirty hands and a dirty face.
2. *Situation:* Jill is playing the stereo exceedingly loud and you have a splitting headache.
3. *Situation:* Eddie and his friend George are playing catch in front of the house. One of them just missed—and the ball went through your living room window.
4. *Situation:* Joan has been on the phone for the last two hours talking to her girlfriends. You are expecting an important business call and you would like to keep the phone free.
5. *Situation:* Your friend whom you haven't seen for several months is visiting you with her three-year-old. The youngster is pulling leaves off your favorite plant.

Part three: ". . . because_____." Now is your chance to express what's happening to *you* as a result of the problem. Again, you can sabotage your whole message if you let supposition, blame or judgment creep in here.

Let's take our two-part messages and try out two "because" statements for each and see if you can choose the one that will work the best.

Situation: Teens are snacking from the minute they come in from school and aren't hungry at dinnertime. They just pick at their food and then are ready to eat again soon after dinner. Parents don't think they are eating enough nutritious food.

Message #1:   "I feel frustrated when no one's hungry at dinnertime and dinner doesn't get eaten, *because I'm concerned about your getting enough nutritious food.*"

Message #2:   "I feel frustrated when no one's hungry at dinnertime and dinner doesn't get eaten, *because I just know you are going to ruin your health with all that junk food!*"

Which message did you choose? Message #1 is great. It will work. By "work" we don't mean that your teens will immediately stop eating between meals. What we do mean is that your teens will usually respond to the message you send them, thereby giving you more information regarding their needs. Now with all of you talking and communicating, the situation can be remedied with good, warm feelings being felt by all family members. Sometimes one STRAIGHT TALK message will get the job done—other times you may need more than one message and/or you may need more than one skill.

Message #2 will probably not work, especially if the issue of "junk food" has been a bone of contention in the past.

Situation: Teenage daughter's room is a sight. You really like a clean house and you have been after your daughter to clean her room for several days now.

Message #1:   "I feel as though I'm not being heard when I say time after time, 'clean your room,' and nothing gets done *because a clean house means an awful lot to me.*"

Message #2: "I feel as though I'm not being heard
when I say time after time, 'clean your
room,' and nothing gets done *because
nobody ever listens to me and I'm sick
and tired of yelling.*"

Which one did you choose? Message #1 is the better
message. Granted, it's a little more risky than Message
#2 because it's revealing two things: that Mom feels
unheard, and that a clean house means an awful lot
to Mom. But, it will usually get you a response and
once communication is in full swing, the situation will
be resolved.

Situation: Your son is a new driver. Dad has allowed him to drive the family car to a
high school dance. He was to be home
by midnight. It is now 2 a.m. and he has
just pulled into the driveway.

Message #1: "I was beside myself with worry when
12:30 came and went and I didn't hear
from you *because I just knew you were
too irresponsible to be trusted with the
good car, especially when you're out
with your wild friends!*"

Message #2: "I was beside myself with worry when
12:30 came and went and I didn't hear
from you *because I was afraid you might
have had an accident and all I could do
was wait!*"

If you chose Message #2, you're doing well. The
"because" phrase in Message #1 ruins the entire statement—it's evaluative and judgmental. The phrase in
Message #2 is very real—it's valid and your teen has
been afraid and many times has had to wait to find
things out, so he is much more likely to respond to the
second message.

There is still one more thing to remember when
sending a Straight Talk I-hurt message (whether that

message is a two-part or a three-part message) and that is: once you have sent your message, you must immediately shift gears and be prepared to use your ATTENTIVE LISTENING skill when the other person replies. The reason for this is that no matter how well we formulate our messages, we're in a conflict area (something is happening that we don't like or something is not happening that we want to happen) and we're confronting the person whom we believe is the culprit. That person is bound to feel some degree of discomfort and since it was our message that produced that discomfort, we must take responsibility for what we have produced and then use our listening skill to help that person voice that discomfort.

This is not as hard to do as you might think. Once you have delivered your message, you will find that your own emotional temperature has leveled off and now you really want to hear what the other person (in this case your son and/or daughter) has to say.

The following Journal Exercise will give you some practice formulating the "because" phrase of a Straight Talk message.

JOURNAL EXERCISE #8

In your Journal write a three-part Straight Talk negative message. These situations are the same as you had in Journal Exercise #6 and #7. Use your "I feel" statements from Exercise #6, and your "when" statements from Exercise #7.

1. *Situation:* Jason comes to the dinner table with dirty hands and a dirty face.
2. *Situation:* Jill is playing the stereo exceedingly loud and you have a splitting headache.
3. *Situation:* Eddie and his friend George are playing catch in front of the house. One of them just missed—and the ball went through your living room window.

4. *Situation:* Joan has been on the phone for the last two hours talking to her girlfriends. You are expecting an important business call and you would like to keep the phone free.

5. *Situation:* Your friend whom you haven't seen for several months is visiting you with her three-year-old. The youngster is pulling leaves off your favorite plant.

Let's go through those three-part messages again and this time we'll add our ATTENTIVE LISTENING skills.

Situation #1:
Teens are snacking from the minute they come in from school and aren't hungry at dinnertime. They just pick at their food and then are ready to eat again soon after dinner. Parents don't think they are eating enough nutritious food.

MOM: (concerned and upset) "I feel frustrated when no one's hungry at dinnertime and dinner doesn't get eaten, because I'm concerned about your getting enough nutritious food." (S-T message)

TEEN: (exasperated) "But we never know what time dinner's going to be—every night it's a different time. All I know is that I'm starving when I get home from school and I've got to eat!"

MOM: (nodding her head) *"You feel hungry* when you come home and having dinner at a different time each night can be a problem." (A-L)

TEEN: (agreeing) "You bet, Mom. Why can't we have a set time for dinner every night, then we'd know how much to eat and still be hungry enough for dinner."

MOM: (still concerned, but agreeing) "Why don't we discuss this at the dinner table tonight? We'll

all be together and then we can talk about the
kinds of snacks you like that Dad and I feel are
nutritious. And we can also discuss regular
dinnertimes."

TEEN: (brightening) "Okay—what time are we having
dinner tonight?"

After Mom sent the initial Straight Talk negative
message, and Teen replied, Mom shifted gears and used
her ATTENTIVE LISTENING skill. When Teen replied again very positively to that statement, Mom
elected to send a more direct statement—this time
following up on a solution offered by Teen (regular
dinnertimes) and then offering a solution herself
(talk about kinds of snacks . . .). All of which, both
Mom and Teen agreed, would be discussed at dinner
tonight. It may be that a few more interchanges at dinner that night will resolve the problem. If not, the whole
subject needs to be aired at a family meeting or at a
contract session—both of which are discussed in depth
in Chapters 8 and 9, respectively.

Situation #2:
Teenage daughter's room is a sight. You really like a
clean house and you have been after your daughter to
clean her room for several days now.

MOM: (frustrated and concerned) "I feel as though
I'm not being heard when I say time after time,
'clean your room,' and nothing gets done because a clean house means an awful lot to me."
(S-T message)

TEEN: (here-we-go-again-attitude) "I know it does,
Mom, but it's my room—why can't I clean it
when *I* want to?"

MOM: (quietly, trying to understand) *"You feel annoyed* when I tell you it's time to clean your
room because this is a decision you want to
make." (A-L)

TEEN: (nodding, agreeing) "That's right, Mom, it would make it more *my* room if *I* could be the one to say when to clean it."

MOM: (understanding, but still troubled) "I can agree with that, but I still need to feel that my house is clean." (S-T message again)

TEEN: (teasingly) "I know, Mom, you're Mrs. Clean, herself. If you didn't yell at me every day to clean my room, I might feel more like doing it."

MOM: (agreeing, yet concerned) *"You feel frustrated* when I tell you every day to clean your room because I haven't really given you an opportunity to make any decisions regarding your room." (A-L)

TEEN: (warming up, a little excited) "I really had some neat ideas on how I wanted to redo my room and you didn't even listen to me when I tried to tell you about them."

MOM: (caring) "What do you say we sit down right now and talk over those ideas and then maybe you can help me with my Mrs. Clean problem."

TEEN: (agreeing, more excited) "Great, Mom. Let's go to my room and talk. Wow, I had just about given up hope on my room!"

Here again, after Mom sent the initial Straight Talk negative message, she used her ATTENTIVE LISTENING skill when Teen replied. When Teen replied the second time, Mom, in addition to her listening skill, again sent a part of her Straight Talk message ". . . but I still need to feel that my house is clean." Once Teen acknowledged she really did hear it, ". . . I know, Mom, you're Mrs. Clean, herself . . .", Mom was able to resume using her listening skill. Next, look what Mom discovered. Mom thought that Teen was not interested in her room at all because she never cleaned it. But, in reality, what Mom discovered was that Teen has some pretty definite ideas on how to fix her room and has been trying to get Mom to listen to her for quite a while.

If Mom can remember here that a Teen is only doing what comes naturally when she wants to be different from her parents, and can let some of that rebellion exert itself in redecorating her room, Mom can then work out a schedule that will be agreeable to both Mom and Teen concerning a clean bedroom. One word of caution here: clean is one thing to Mom and an altogether different thing to Teen. Mom and daughter have to define clean in a way that is agreeable to them both.

Situation #3:

Your son is a new driver. Dad has allowed him to drive the family car to a high school dance. He was to be home by midnight. It is now 2 a.m. and he has just pulled into the driveway.

DAD: (worried and concerned) "I was beside myself with worry when 12:30 came and went and I didn't hear from you, because I was afraid you might have had an accident and all I could do was wait!" (S-T Message)

TEEN: (contrite and concerned) "Gosh, Dad, I'm really sorry. I never thought you'd worry—I knew I could take care of myself, but Jerry got bombed out of his mind and he had his father's car, too, so I did what I thought was right."

DAD: (trying to understand) *"You were feeling responsible* for Jerry." (A-L)

TEEN: (still concerned) "Yeah, I knew his father would ground him for life if anything happened to the car. And boy, Jerry was in no condition to drive."

DAD: (concerned and worried) *"You were really worried* about Jerry." (A-L)

TEEN: (starting to relax) "Yeah. Some guys brought a couple of gallons of wine to the dance at school and sneaked them into the john. Jerry was drinking quite a bit of the wine and all of a sudden just started to doze off. By the end of the dance the P.E. teacher had caught the guys and what was left of the wine and they were suspended on the spot. I didn't want any of the teachers to see Jerry, so we sneaked him out when the dance was over and after I took the others home, I drove Jerry home."

DAD: (still concerned, but relaxing a little) "I imagine Jerry's father was pretty worried, too."

TEEN: (relaxed now) "He sure was—but I think he was more worried about the car because he called Jerry every name he could think of for getting drunk and taking a chance on almost wrecking his car. Well, I offered to take Jerry's father to the school so he could pick up his car. I knew Jerry would get it even worse if something happened to that car sitting all alone in the parking lot overnight. After I dropped him off at his car I came right home."

DAD: (smiling, lovingly) "It's been quite an evening. *I'm really proud of the way you handled things, son.* You did what was best for everyone concerned." (S-T positive message)

TEEN: (concerned) "Yeah, Dad—except for you and Mom. I guess I'm going to be grounded for a while for getting home so late."

DAD: (warmly) "No, son, I don't think so. We should have discussed what to do in emergencies such as this one before you left tonight. Why don't we talk a little bit more tomorrow after we've both had some sleep. I'm certain we can come up with a game plan for emergencies that will make us both happy."

TEEN: (happily) "Boy, Dad, I'm glad I'm me and have you for a father and not Jerry. Thanks, Dad, see you tomorrow."

Dad sent a Straight Talk I-hurt-message and Teen replied. Then Dad continued using his ATTENTIVE LISTENING skill. After Teen finishes relating what happened, Dad is able to sum up the evening and compliment his son on the way he handled things. By doing that, the son is able to see the missing link—which is the fact that Mom and Dad put in some hours of unneeded worry. The final statement made by Dad shows him to be very human—even parents with much experience make mistakes or omit things. We're willing to bet you that everyone slept better in this household than in Jerry's household the night of the infamous dance!

JOURNAL EXERCISE #9

Choose three specific situations and send a Straight Talk I-hurt-message. Write out in your Journal the situation, your two- or three-part Straight Talk message, your teen's response, and your response. This last response will be your ATTENTIVE LISTENING response.

1. Situation.
2. Two- or three-part Straight Talk Message.
3. Teen's response.
4. Your ATTENTIVE LISTENING response.

CHAPTER 6

Praise/Criticism

Praise and criticism are two sides of the same coin

As parents, we may find it comparatively easy to praise a young child, but exceedingly difficult to praise a teenager. For most parents most of the time, children are a lot easier to live with than teenagers. Parents usually "win" conflicts involving young children. We have a lot of "power" over young children because they need and depend upon us so much. But with teens, it's exactly the opposite. They are sometimes very difficult to like. Invariably parents "lose" conflicts involving their teenagers. And what really hurts parents is the realization that they have lost most of the power they used to have now that their adorable baby has suddenly, overnight, blossomed into a teenager untouchable! In addition to this "lost" power a parent finds it hard, if not impossible, to allow a teen to make a wrong decision. A parent finds it difficult to trust that his teen can learn from his mistakes and make better decisions in the future. So, once again, we do what we know best—we criticize, and think for our teen. If it was good enough for our parents, most of us find it's good enough for us. Right? WRONG! As teenagers most of us experienced the same routine that we are passing on to *our* teenagers. As parents we are also reacting to our teens in a way we have heard, and sometimes read, others react:

"The teen years are intolerable . . ."

"Live through them as well as you can . . ."

"Keep your teenager in line as best you can . . ."

"No love is possible during this trying time . . ."

"They usually straighten out by the time they're twenty-five years old . . ."

"Parents of teens are to be pitied . . ."

"Teens don't know the words 'gratitude' or "appreciation' . . ."

These and more little "truths" are all part of our accumulated culture. We are frightened into believing that this is the way it probably will be. We expect it to happen and by golly, it does!

Why aren't we told that being a teenager today is full of pitfalls? Why aren't we told that parents are just as important during this period of a youngster's life as they ever were? Why aren't we told that teens need parents now, too? Why aren't we told what to do and what to expect and how to handle problems as they arise? In other words, how to live and enjoy these precious, so very important teenage years?

One reason is that it takes a very long time to change ways of doing things. But there have been a few voices trying to make changes—Dr. Haim Ginot, Dr. Thomas Gordon, Dr. Fitzhugh Dobson, yes, and even Ann Landers and Dear Abby. But change takes time. There also has to be a reason for change—and you, the reader, know that more than anyone else. You want a change—that's why you're reading this book.

Praise from parents is a necessary and vital need of the adolescent. Some parents think all they need to provide for their teen is food, shelter, and clothing; and if they do these three things, they believe they are doing an excellent job as parents. Wrong!

Unfortunately, many parents don't know how to use or give praise simply because they rarely received enough praise when they were teens.

To begin with, promise yourself that from this day forward, you will try not to criticize in a destructive way, and that you will try to praise your teen often.

PRAISE

Let's talk about praise first. In Chapter 5, we discussed in depth the Straight-Talk I-hurt (negative feeling message) skill. When you want to praise someone use your Straight-Talk I-love or I-am-happy skill (positive feeling message). I feel *(a positive feeling word)* when *(describe what's happening or not happening to make you feel good—the pronoun "you" may be used here)* because *(tell why that makes you feel good)*.

I-AM-HAPPY (POSITIVE FEELING) MESSAGE

Let's look at what happens when you send a message like the one described above. First of all, it tells how you feel about something—you're sharing something with your teen. Believe it or not, your teen wants you to feel happy, but that is not his first priority, so he may not get to it very often.

Secondly, this message describes a situation or a happening that is positive, and because your teen is involved in that positive action, he feels a glow of self-esteem.

Teens need to feel that they are capable of more positive actions than negative ones. They need to feel they are "good" people, that there is a reason for their being, that they are meeting some expectations—of both their own and their parents.

For example, Johnny's chore is putting the garbage cans at the curb each Tuesday evening for the garbage truck pick up early Wednesday morning. For the last several weeks, he has had to be hounded to put out the garbage cans. This week, outside of a gentle reminder, the parents have decided not to do any hounding or hassling. After dinner, Dad casually mentions that tonight is Tuesday night, and the garbage man comes tomorrow. At about 8:30 p.m., Johnny goes outside and takes the garbage cans to the curb. What can Dad say? His message does not have to be a sophisticated one, it can be as simple as the following one:

"I really felt good when the garbage cans were taken out tonight without any hassle because I know what a nuisance job they can be. Thanks, Johnny!"

It would certainly be appropriate for Dad to smile and put his arm around Johnny's shoulders while he's sending the above message.

Dad's message stated the situation and when it took place ("when the garbage cans were taken out tonight . . ."). In other words, Johnny is being praised for a specific action and that action is tied to a specific time ". . . tonight . . ." Johnny can accept this statement of praise, without feeling guilty, because it states a fact.

Praise is like icing on a cake. Too much of it can be sickening, not enough of it makes the cake unappealing.

Don't expect any more of a response from Johnny than, "Yeah," "Okay, Dad," "Sure, I know," or just a grunt. As a parent, your job was done and it was done well when you sent your message. Granted, you might have wanted a reply from Johnny like: "It's okay, Dad, I really need to help you more around here." But, remember, Rome wasn't built in a day and a reply like that will take a little while in coming, if ever!

Try to remember that one positive exchange builds on another. In the beginning it's a slow, agonizing long road.

Sometimes it's hard for parents to see anything in a positive light where their teens are concerned. Many parents get into a rut of criticism and let the few positive actions pass by with no comment and come down heavy on the negative actions with truckloads of criticism.

EXAMPLE #1:

Teen comes home at the designated time after a dance at school, even though his car broke down.

Straight Talk Positive Messages:
"I feel good when a commitment we made together is kept because I know you had to make a special effort tonight to keep it."

"Wow, I'm glad you're home because I was worried when I found out your car broke down." (Remember, this three-part message is interchangeable—you can start your message with "I feel" or "Because" or "When." The formula "I feel _____ when _____ because _____" is only to help you compose your beginning messages.)

EXAMPLE #2:

Your teen's report card shows marked improvement in one or more subjects.

Straight Talk Positive Messages:
"I feel really proud when I see that chemistry mark go from a D+ to a B— because I know how hard you worked to make that change happen."

"When your report card came in the mail today, and I saw that B— in Chemistry, I couldn't wait until you got home to tell you what a great job you did and how proud I am of you. I think that calls for a celebration so I'm making your favorite dessert for dinner tonight!"

How many mothers would have thought of that

special, something extra? What's wrong with a special surprise, a reward for a job well done? Nothing! Your teen undoubtedly put himself out to get that B— in chemistry. The very least a parent can do is to take as much note of that B— as she did of the D+!

EXAMPLE #3:

Your teen, after practicing every day for weeks on end, made the varsity team.

Straight Talk Positive Messages:

"I was so excited when I found out that you made the varsity team because I know how very hard you worked to make that happen. Congratulations, son."

"When I found out that you made the varsity team, I just beamed from ear to ear because I know the time and effort you put forth to make it."

It would be a good idea, too, to follow up that statement by going to as many of his games as you can and cheering for the home team.

A happy, close-knit family uses lots of praise.

We have had parents, fathers especially, say, "When he's doing something wrong, I tell him—when I don't say anything, he knows he's doing something right!" The poor children in that family—they may very well turn out to be bankrupt—emotionally. The teens in that family will only experience criticism, which always produces feelings of inadequacy, hurt, and failure. Praise, on the other hand, produces feelings of high self-esteem, success, warmth and caring. If all our children learn from us is how to criticize, then they have every right to feel short-changed.

A home, especially for a teen, needs to be a place of refuge, a place of learning, a place of caring, a place of acceptance. Praise helps make a home all these things.

The following Journal Exercise will help you become aware of the opportunities you had to praise your teen but didn't.

JOURNAL EXERCISE #10

In your Journal, list three different situations where you honestly could have praised your teen but did not. Write out the situation and then a two- or three-part Straight Talk Positive Message for each situation.

1. Write out three different situations.
2. After each, write a Straight Talk Positive Message.

CRITICISM

Now for a word about criticism. If you could find a recipe for a happy home, it would call for just a pinch of constructive criticism. Most homes today shovel it out by the truckload!

Here are some helpful hints for using constructive criticism:

1. Never citicize the person. Criticizing the person lowers that person's self-esteem, his feeling of self-worth. Separate the behavior from the person and send a Straight-Talk Negative Message that tells how you feel about the behavior.
2. The behavior, the situation, what's happening or not happening may be criticized, but remember your message should only contain the present behavior or situation. Don't use this opoprtunity to throw everything but the kitchen sink into your message.

For example, Tim is showing his son, Andy, how to hang doors. Tim gives Andy a careful explanation of what's to be done next. Andy starts to pick up the wrong size tool for the job.

Wrong:

TIM: "You never get anything right, Andy. You don't listen to what I'm saying. No wonder you're flunking algebra. You're just a dumb, lazy kid!"

Correct:

TIM: "Here's the right size tool, Andy. Try this one."

Another alternative might be to let Andy complete the job (if possible) with the tool he chooses and then discuss the pros and cons of which tool does the better job.

In the first example above, Andy will tune out his father's voice, because he knows what's coming. Parents think kids don't hear them so they repeat things over and over again and it's like talking into a dead phone. In this case, Andy's been through this dialogue a dozen times—he knows what's coming next, so he just tunes out. Tim attacks Andy as a person. The end result will be that Andy will continue to act like a "dumb, lazy kid" because that is the only way he can get back at his father for calling him names and making him feel stupid, unimportant and not worth much.

In the second example above, Jim is modeling patience as well as help. If Tim follows the second alternative, he may find that several size tools can do the job—at least he will be giving his son the feeling that he (the son) is a person important enough to be listened to.

It's not easy to take criticism, no matter where it comes from. But if the criticism can be leveled against the action and not the person, it can be considered to be constructive criticism. When the person is criticized (as in the first example above), the criticism is destructive.

> *When a teen is surrounded by criticism, his out-look on life is a negative one. When a teen is surrounded by praise, his outlook on life is a positive one.*

Obviously, other factors enter into a teen's outlook on life in addition to criticism and praise; however, we can't emphasize enough the importance of praise and the negative effects of destructive criticism.

The following Journal Exercise will help you become aware of the number of times you use criticism and whether you use constructive or destructive criticism. It will also give you another chance to practice your Straight-Talk Negative Message Skill.

JOURNAL EXERCISE #11
   In your Journal, list three different situations in which you criticized your teen. Write out the situation, your message to your teen, and whether or not you used constructive or destructive criticism. Finally, for each situation, compose a two- or three-part Straight Talk Negative Message.
1. Write out three different situations.
2. Write your reply for each.
3. Identify whether or not your criticism was constructive or destructive.
4. Write a Straight Talk Negative Message for each situtaion.

Remember the old adage, "You can catch more flies with honey than with vinegar." Try it, it works!

CHAPTER 7

T & T Contact
(Time and Touch)

Adolescents need contact with their parents. This contact needs to be in terms of time and in terms of touching.

TIME

Time is getting to be a more precious commodity today than gold! In the life of a teenager, it is even more precious. Parents need to plan their schedules to include this very important time with their teenagers. Parents will say—especially fathers—"I don't have anything in common with my son (or daughter). I don't know how to relate to him (or her)."

Most likely, these parents had little time spent with them by their parents. They have not acquired any skills in relating to their own teens. But remember, skills can be learned. You've already made the first step when you completed Journal Exercise #10 which had you list three situations where you could have praised your teen. You've also learned how to listen and talk with your teen. Now all you have to do is to find the time to translate that approval (praise) and interest in listening and talking with your teen and you've made a giant stride toward a better relationship with your teen.

In our busy, busy world, most of us, including parents, complain that there is never enough time to do all the things we need to do and all the things we want to do. When times becomes short, we always try to fit in some of the things we *want* to do even if that means foregoing one or two things we know we really *should* do. Sometimes one of the first things to go will be the time we meant to spend with our teenager. It's easy to see how that could happen. Even though you spent considerable time with your youngster when he was growing up, it may be that now you have to work harder and harder to get your teen to spend some time with you, especially since his peer group becomes his primary source of feedback and approval.

When you get a few turn-downs, you might very probably say to yourselves, "Well, I've got other things I really want to be doing, too." And that same bit of time that you might have spent with your teen is instead spent working on your tax return, or writing checks to pay bills, or watching a rerun of the football game of the century! Before you know it, after enough turn-downs, parents just stop asking! And that's a mistake. It is important to keep asking.

Keep offering to spend time with your teen—at least your teen will be aware that you're there and you're available—that alone will give him the sense of family that's so important to teens.

Try to think of things to do with your teen that you both enjoy, things that you know he's enjoyed in the past. Be aware of what his current interests are. Most important, try not to feel resentful, rejected, or unhappy when your teen turns down your offer to spend time with him—at least you're keeping the doors of communication open and your teen knows that if he needs you, you're there.

Time spent with your teen fulfills two needs:
1. The need for a role model.
For each boy, the primary role model of a man is

his father. For a girl, the primary role model of a woman is her mother. Conversely, a boy's primary role of a woman is his mother and a girl's primary role model of a man is her father. So the time each of you spend with your children is important —especially for your teens. It helps them to define their own sex roles and identities, as well as learn to relate to opposite sex role models.

2. The need for building self-esteem.

The quality of time you spend with your teens is much more important than the quantity of time. You can enhance the quality of that time by reviewing and building on those things you like about your teen.

If one of the things a father likes about his son is the fact that his son is interested in sports, the father might spend a little time discussing a professional game that was televised. Or, he might suggest that he and his son attend a game. If his son likes that idea, he should quickly make the appropriate arrangements and once at the game, give his attention to his son as well as the game. Listen to what your son has to say about the players, ask him questions, show him by your actions and your words that he is important to you. Before the evening is over, tell him you really liked being with him and suggest you both do it again soon.

If one of the things a mother likes about her daughter is the fact that she loves clothes, she might spend a little time discussing styles of clothes and suggest a trip to a special store to check out styles and perhaps buy some things. Make it an all-day affair with lunch at a very special place. Show your daughter by your words and your actions that you are enjoying the time together.

Also, mothers need to find time to spend with their sons, and fathers need to find time to spend with their daughters.

That's what we mean by time contact. Not only time spent together, but time spent meaningfully together with interaction on both sides.

If your teen is declining your offers to spend time with him, don't give up. How would you handle a difficult person you were doing business with? If you are a salesman and you had a client who turned you down again and again, would you give up? It would probably present you with a challenge, and you'd keep after that person until you made your sale. If you work in an office and a project you're working on doesn't go smoothly at first, would you throw out the idea or would you keep working on it until it was just right? If you're an auto mechanic repairing a car and things don't go right at first, would you give up? If you're sewing a new outfit and you were having difficulty fitting a sleeve, would you leave it unfinished? Well, try these same tactics with your son or daughter. Consider it a challenge and if things don't go smoothly at first, hang in there!

The following Journal Exercise will help you become aware of the time you spend *alone* with your teenager.

JOURNAL EXERCISE #12

In your Journal for one week's duration, write down how much time you spend alone with each of your teens.
1. Name of teen.
2. When time was spent.
3. Duration of "alone" time with your teen.
4. Subject(s) discussed.

TOUCHING

Touching is a lost art! And that's a pity! All human beings need touching. When they don't get enough of it, they wither, lose self-esteem and become alienated people. We usually don't touch youngsters past the baby stage and the little boy and little girl stages—and that's too bad.

So often touching is viewed as sexual, and while touching can indeed be a very satisfying, fulfilling sexual experience, it doesn't have to be. Touching is a healthy, loving (but not always sexual), satisfying, pleasurable means of communication that has been dreadfully neglected over the years.

A touch can say, "I care," "I like you," "I love you," "I'm here," and many, many more things.

If you have not been a "touching" family when your children were younger, it's going to be difficult for you to start now. But remember, there are degrees of touching. Hugging is touching; so is a handshake or a pat on the shoulder. Don't think that you have to go overboard to start. Your teen would think you a bit strange if you went from "no touching" to repeated bear hugs! Look for occasions where a touch is appropriate for you. If you are going to be embarrassed when you're touching, your teen will be embarrassed also. Touching is a very personal thing—you must be comfortable doing it.

Take your time, find a way that's comfortable for you, and while you're seeking ways to touch that seem right to you, spend your time keeping the communication channels open between you and your teen.

The following Journal Exercise will help you become aware of the times you touch your teens over a period of a week.

JOURNAL EXERCISE #13

In your Journal for one week's duration, write down the number of times you touched your teens.

1. Name of teen.
2. When you touched your teen.
3. Describe the touch (ex. handshake, bear hug, etc.)
4. Teen's reaction.

CHAPTER 8

Family Problem-Solving Meeting

Whenever two or more people live together under the same roof, there are bound to be disagreements—some small, some horrendous! Add to that an adolescent or two and those disagreements can turn into pandemonium.

If these disagreements or clashes are not brought out into the open and all parties concerned do not discuss the problem openly, and no solution is sought, then resentment, anger and frustration become a part of daily living in that household.

The basic skills you have now learned (ATTENTIVE LISTENING and STRAIGHT TALK) will help you avoid many of the clashes you have had in the past with your teen. These two skills alone will help to lower emotional temperatures when they start to climb. Just talking and listening to each other will help each of you unload some of the frustration, dissatisfaction and weariness we all experience—both young people and adults—in day-to-day living.

But because each of you in a household is a distinct, separate entity, there are certainly going to be disagreements, clashes and problems. At least now you have a base of concern and caring feelings that will bring you together, so that these disagreements, clashes and problems can be handled. Sometimes the outcomes will be creative solutions and at other times the outcomes will be compromised/negotiated solutions. The skills you use will be the same for either outcome.

CREATIVE SOLUTIONS

When a need exists that doesn't threaten the values of the household, the meeting of that need can most frequently fall under the heading of "creative solution." A creative solution is one where everyone involved feels they have won.

COMPROMISED/NEGOTIATED SOLUTIONS

When a need exists that does threaten the values of the household, the outcome here most frequently would fall under the heading of "compromised/negotiated solution." A compromised/negotiated solution is one where everyone involved feels that they have lost a little, but they can live with the solution.

The feeling you get after the solution has been agreed upon is what tells you whether the solution was a creative one or a compromised/negotiated one.

This chapter may very well be the hardest to understand and the hardest to put into practice. Parents who have mastered these skills and use them report extraordinary results. The next chapter on the *Contract Problem-Solving Meeting* serves the same purpose as this chapter. Use whichever method feels right for you—the one that best fits your parenting style. Both produce excellent results. The choice is yours.

PROBLEM-SOLVING PROCESS

Your STRAIGHT TALK skill is needed so that you can define the problem and your ATTENTIVE LISTENING skill is needed so that you can understand how the other person views the problem.

To these skills you now add *Brainstorming*.

Brainstorming is fun and once the ground rules are

set, participants enjoy the skill. The ground rules are simple:

1. Everyone's idea is worthy of consideration.
2. Do not negatively evaluate or put down any person's idea.
3. Do not negatively evaluate or put down any person.

Businesses, industry, government and school districts all use Brainstorming to generate many solutions to different problems. Once all parties concerned are aware of the many approaches to a specific problem, the choosing of one or more solutions that are agreeable to all parties becomes an easier chore.

For example, you own a restaurant and Tuesday is your slowest day. You call together your top people and tell them the problem: Tuesday is a slow business day and you want to do something to increase business on that day. Do they have any ideas? Alone, you may be able to generate five or six ideas, but with others, your group will probably generate five, ten, twenty times as many ideas. And from that larger source, those of you who will be responsible for promoting those ideas can choose appropriately and intelligently.

For this brainstorming meeting, you have asked the following people to attend: your business partner, the maitre d', the chief chef, the head waitress, and your accountant. Why did you ask all these people? Realistically, the only person you have to consult is your business partner and maybe your accountant. However, it would be wise to keep in mind that whatever ideas result from this brainstorming meeting will only be as successful as the people who will carry out these ideas. Big business found out a long time ago that when people feel a part of something, they are more likely to make that something a success.

So, as a restaurant owner, you know that by inviting the key people in your business operation to brainstorm ideas on how to increase business on Tuesdays, your chances of success will be greatly enhanced.

Below are some ideas that might possibly evolve from such a meeting. Remember now, all of these ideas were offered by the people at your meeting and the one thing you impressed upon your group were the three ground rules of brainstorming.

1. Encourage service clubs to meet at your restaurant on Tuesdays.
2. Have Tuesday Specials.
3. Encourage family night on Tuesdays with special prices for children and large groups.
4. Cut the staff on Tuesdays so the overhead is not so high.
5. Advertise more in newspapers and on the radio.
6. Sell dine-out cards good only on Tuesdays.
7. Make Tuesdays theme days. One week have Chinese cooking, another week have Greek cooking, etc., and have the staff dress the part.
8. Make Tuesdays teenage Disco Night.
9. Close on Tuesdays.
10. Have Senior Citizens' Specials on Tuesday afternoons and evenings.

The participants at your meeting may very well choose several of the above ideas. You, your partner and your accountant will be able to discuss the reality of each of them in terms of money, time, etc., but those that are finally chosen have a better chance of succeeding because each key person in your organization has had a voice in the decision-making process. When a person has a voice in the decision-making process, he is much more likely to feel a responsibility to shoulder his share.

These same concepts can work at home. It's a little harder to do because at home when problems arise emotions also rise and we sometimes find it hard to "stick to the facts." If we take care of the emotions first, then we can get down to the business of "the facts."

For example, when your teen has just totaled the family car, when the police have called to tell you to come to the station to pick up your daughter, when the school has just notified you that your teen has cut class for the last two weeks—these emotions need to be taken care of first. It may very well take several meetings with your teen to deal with the emotions present. But only after that is done can you sit down together and discuss what can be done about the problem.

Are we talking about a family meeting? Yes, in a way. It is a meeting and it does include family members. But there the similarity stops. You have communication skills now—your ATTENTIVE LISTENING skill, your STRAIGHT TALK skill and your BRAINSTORMING skill.

Now, each family member can look at the problem with an open mind, and while emotions are bound to be present, they will not block the way of finding a solution acceptable to all and therefore workable.

By using your skills, you are building a climate of trust and caring, and that trust and caring is a two-way street, your trusting and caring for your adolescent and his trusting and caring for you.

Let's take one of the situations above and discuss it in terms of the new skill you have learned.

SITUATION:

Jim, your 16½-year-old has been driving for six months and occasionally you allow him to use the big family car which is only a year old. He had permission to use the family car today for a special school affair. You have just been told that your new car is totaled.

This situation will evoke several emotions: anger (certainly!), frustration (probably!), concern for your teen's well-being (definitely!). It may take several give and take meetings between you and your teen to talk through these emotions. (In Chapter 11 we discuss anger in depth, and we suggest that you read this chapter before putting into practice the skills in this and the following chapter.)

Remember, also, that your teen is experiencing several emotions: anger (a more helpless kind of anger which can be devastating when turned inward or against oneself), frustration (aimed not only at himself, but the situation, too), concern for his parents and himself (how are his parents going to weather this latest storm and how will it affect him). So, you can see that the emotions match—both parents and teen need to "clear the air" before the nitty-gritty problems generated by this accident can be solved. As you use your ATTENTIVE LISTENING skill and your STRAIGHT TALK skill, you will find emotional temperatures declining, tempers settling, and concern for each family member taking hold again. Now is the time to come together and solve the problem confronting the family.

SITUATION:

The counselor at school has just notified you that Jerry, your 15-year-old son, has been cutting classes for the last two weeks. You were under the impression that he had been in school all day for the two weeks in question.

First you take care of the emotions involved here— probably concern, worry, fear, etc. Then, you and Jerry can look at the problem. What that problem or problems might be would depend on the individual family. Has this happened before? What were the circumstances? And so forth. Most likely the problems would fall within the following general areas:

1. Why has Jerry been cutting classes?
2. What was he getting out of cutting classes?
3. Where was Jerry during this time?

4. What was he doing?
5. What will these cuts do to Jerry's grades?
6. How can the problem(s) be resolved?

Keep in mind that your teen needs to be a full-fledged member of this family meeting, and as such has a responsibility (as do the parents) to do what he can to help the family through this difficulty. Each person needs to be heard, both in putting forth the problem and in brainstorming solutions to the problem. Once the problem is fully stated, it is time to start BRAINSTORMING.

When the BRAINSTORMING is completed—and that usually happens when everybody just runs out of ideas, then it's time to choose solutions from the list generated, so it is important to see that someone records the solutions as they are given.

Making our choices of solutions means only a simple declaration of "I like the second solution and the eighth solution. I don't like the seventh and the ninth solutions." Each participant gets an opportunity to discuss each suggestion. As soon as a solution is eliminated by a person, draw a line through it. The solutions remaining are agreeable to all family members. Choose them all or decide as a group that you will only choose numbers two and three, etc.

Now, all you have left to do is to determine who does what and when; and set up a follow-up meeting.

Let's make this process more specific for you and show you step-by-step what is involved.

1. *Schedule a time to meet.*

   When a problem or difficulty has surfaced between family members, a meeting time and place should be set. This meeting should include only those people involved in the problem or who are affected by the problem. The meeting time and place should be agreeable to all participants.

2. *Define the problem or situation.*

   Everyone at the meeting gets an opportunity to

state the problem as he perceives it. Use your STRAIGHT TALK skill to present your definition of the problem and your ATTENTIVE LISTENING skill to help the others state the problem as they perceive it. This talking-out stage is the most important step, so spend the time you need to give everyone present an opporunity to be heard. If this step is hurried or is incomplete, the whole process will collapse at Step 5.

3. *Choose a recorder.*

Ask one in the group to volunteer to be the recorder. If no one wants to volunteer, ask the group if they would feel comfortable having you as the recorder.

4. *Brainstorm solutions.*

Follow the three ground rules:

1. Everyone's idea is worthy of consideration.
2. Do not negatively evaluate or put down any person's idea.
3. Do not negatively evaluate or put down any person.

Continue this step until ideas stop flowing. It's going to take vigilance on your part to see that each person's ideas are accepted and not evaluated. Evaluation and creativity cannot co-exist. Nothing dries up creativity faster than evaluation and criticism.

5. *Review the solutions.*

This is the failsafe step. Everyone gets an opportunity to review the list of solutions generated. As soon as someone rejects a solution, eliminate that solution. Draw a line through each solution as it is eliminated. Your list should include one or more solutions that are acceptable to all members of the group. If so, go to Step 6. (If all the solutions were rejected, the problem was not fully defined and you need to go back to Step 1. If you go through this process again, and again all solutions were rejected, we suggest you use the Contract Problem-Solving skill outlined in the following chapter.)

6. *Making a choice.*

As a group, determine which of the acceptable solutions you are going to use. You may want to use them all; you may discover that two are almost alike; or you may decide to choose only one solution.

7. *Fill in the four "W's."*

*W*ho does *w*hat by *w*hen and *w*here. In order to implement the choices made, certain things may have to be done. Ask for volunteers and see that each person understands the assignment he chooses.

8. *Follow-up.*

Before you adjourn the family meeting, set up a time ten days or two weeks in the future so that everyone can report on how the solutions chosen are working. If they're not doing too well, go through the process again and find better solutions to the problem.

A family meeting has a much better chance of success if communication skills have been used for a period of time. If you try it at the beginning, you may find that your teen will view the whole process as another gimmick and will drag his feet all the way. Wait until the family climate is good—you are the best judge of when that is—and then you can undertake such a meeting.

Following is an example of a family meeting.

SITUATION:

Every Sunday your family goes to your husband's parents' home for lunch. This has been a family ritual for years now. Recently, 14-year-old Jerry has not wanted to go. You've tried everything you can think of to get him to go. Most of the time he stays home anyway—and when he does go, he ruins everybody's day.

1. *Schedule a time to meet.*

   This meeting will include Jerry, his Dad and his Mom. The meeting time and place must be agreeable to the three of them.

2. *Define the problem or situation.*

   Using your STRAIGHT TALK message skill and your ATTENTIVE LISTENING skill, the following concerns have surfaced.

MOM: Wants to continue this family ritual. It's important to her that her family enjoy each other's company.

DAD: Wants to spend time with his parents as well as his family. Sunday is the one day he can do this. Saturday is reserved for chores around the house and he strongly believes Sunday should be devoted to family activities and that these activities should include lunch at his parents' home.

JERRY: Really enjoys his grandparents but doesn't want to go to lunch there every Sunday. He wants to do less with his family and spend more time with his friends. He wants time to be alone in his room and he wants to listen to his stereo.

3. *Choose a recorder.*

   Jerry volunteers to be a recorder.

4. *Brainstorm solutions.*

   The participants—Mom, Dad and Jerry—follow the three ground rules for brainstorming and suggest the following ideas.

   1. Jerry goes to his grandparents' home for lunch twice a month. Jerry chooses which times.

   2. Jerry goes each week but doesn't have to stay for lunch.

   3. Mom plans other family activities for Sundays every now and then.

4. Dad does some of the Saturday-chore-work in the evening during the week which will free some time for Saturday family activities.

5. Go fishing as a family.

6. Spend a day in the desert and look for rocks and explore caves.

7. Don't do anything on Sunday.

8. Mom and Dad will go to grandparents' home each Sunday for lunch alone.

9. Ask Jerry's friends to go with the family to grandparents' every so often.

10. Every other week have grandparents over to our home.

11. Arrange time for Jerry to have the house all to himself each week—for a couple of hours—so he can really listen to his stereo the way he likes to.

12. Jerry can visit his grandparents by himself besides Sundays.

5. *Review the solutions.*

MOM: "I like ideas #1, #3, #4, #6, #9, #10, #11, & #12. I don't like #2, #5, #7 & #8."

DAD: "I like #1, #3, #4, #10, #11,& #12. I don't like #4 & #9."

JERRY: "I like #1, #3, #6, #10, #11, & #12. All the ones I don't like are already crossed out."

6. *Making a choice.*

Jerry's list now looks like this:

1. Jerry goes to his grandparents' home for lunch twice a month. Jerry chooses which times.

2. ~~Jerry goes each week but doesn't have to stay for lunch.~~

3. Mom plans other family activities for Sundays every now and then.

4. ~~Dad does some of the Saturday-chore-work in the evening during the week which will free some time for Saturday family activities.~~

5. ~~Go fishing as a family.~~

6. Spend a day in the desert and look for rocks and explore caves.

7. ~~Don't do anything on Sunday.~~

8. ~~Mom and Dad go to grandparents' home each Sunday for lunch alone.~~

9. ~~Ask Jerry's friends to go with the family to grandparents' every so often.~~

10. Every other week have grandparents over to our house.

11. Arrange for Jerry to have the house all to himself each week—for a couple of hours—so he can really listen to his stereo the way he likes to.

12. Jerry can visit his grandparents by himself besides Sundays.

Solutions #1, #3, #6, #10, #11 & #12 remain.

DAD: "They all look good to me. #10 may not be too good because Grandmom and Grandpop have trouble moving about, but I'll ask them and see what happens."

MOM: "I like all of them, too."

JERRY: "Me, too, especially #11!"

7. *Fill in the four "W's".*

Who does What by When and Where?

DAD: "I'll check out #10 with Mom and Dad— I'll do that before next Sunday."

JERRY: "I'll choose my twice a month dates ahead of time and let you know what they are. I'll also check with Grandmom and Grandpop about the best times for me to drop by."

MOM: "Fine. I'll start planning a day at the desert. Also, Jerry, I've been thinking about some time for you to have in the house alone. How about if we try out the evening Dad and I go shopping. We're gone every Wednesday evening for about two hours. How does that sound?"

JERRY: "Just great, Mom! Let's start these ideas right away!"

8. *Follow-up.*

DAD: "Before we finish, let's set a time to meet in about ten days. That will be Monday, April 4th. Is that convenient for everyone?"

Is this a creative solution or a compromised/negotiated solution? Could be either. If each believes they've won—and we think Mom, Dad and Jerry believe they have—it's a creative solution. If each believes they've lost a little—then it's a compromised/negotiated solution.

The family meeting problem-solving process works well in families where parents share responsibility (and power). If as a parent you find you need to have more control of the process, the contract problem-solving process may be more compatible to your parenting style.

CHAPTER 9

The Contract Problem-Solving Meeting

The contract problem-solving meeting is another way of settling differences between adolescents and parents. The contract meeting involves a greater risk than the family meeting because the parents evaluate the teen's behaviors and the teen evaluates the parents' behaviors.

However, for some families it may be the better way to resolve differences.

When using the contract method, three things must be present:
1. Both parents and teen must be willing to make some changes. That means both of you must be willing to negotiate and compromise.
2. Both parents and teen must come together in good faith, with good will and a positive attitude that the process will work.
3. Both parents and teen must agree to try not to hurt each other.

Make it clear at the beginning that the purpose of the contract meeting is to change behavior—both on the part of the parents and on the part of the teen. All parties must understand that the outcome of a contract meeting is a two-way contract—both parents and teen will be expected to change some behaviors.

83

1. *Set a meeting time.*
Set a time for your contract problem-solving meeting. Meeting time and place must be agreeable to parents and teen. You will need privacy—a place away from other family members where you will not be disturbed throughout the meeting. Meeting participants will be one parent and one teen or two parents and one teen. Have pencils and paper available.

2. *List behaviors each wants the other to change.*
Each of you make a list of the behaviors you want the other to change. Teen makes his list of behaviors he would like parent(s) to change. Parents, working together, make a list of behaviors they want teen to change. Allow ten minutes only for this step. (Make certain your list includes only behaviors, not personality traits. Behaviors would be: didn't empty the garbage last night; or teased his younger sister today; or forgot to feed the dog yesterday. Personality traits would be: he doesn't laugh enough; or he's always depressed; or he's too quiet.)
Choose three behaviors you want to discuss at this contract meeting. Put checks by those three behaviors.

3. *List behaviors each wants the other to keep.*
On another sheet, each of you make a list of the behaviors you like and want the other person to keep. Here again, teen makes his list and parents, working together, make their list of behaviors they like about their teen and want him to keep. Allow ten minutes only for this step.

4. *Discussion of the "Don'ts" in Step 2.*
Parents and teen come together now with the understanding that each will be honest and forthright with each other. The intent here is to learn to work together—each of you must try to be careful that no one is hurt in the process.
Flip a coin to determine who starts the discussion.

If your teen wins the toss of the coin, he makes the first request for change to his parents. The parents then repeat what they heard their teen say to make sure they've heard it correctly and that they understand teen's request. When the teen agrees that they have, then the parents say, "yes," or "no," or they offer the teen a compromise. The parents may want to discuss the issue a bit before answering and if that's the case, the discussion should take place right there and an answer given to teen immediately after the discussion. If the parents answer "yes," the requested behavior is written on a sheet of paper and both parent(s) and teen sign their names.

If a compromised solution is agreed to, the parents write down the compromised solution on a piece of paper and parent(s) and teen sign their names to it.

If the parents answer "no," teen accepts the answer. Now, it's the parents turn. They read a behavior they want their teen to change. Teen repeats what he has heard to make sure he understands and has accurately heard the request. Teen now has an opportunity to respond with a "yes," "no," or teen may offer parents a compromise. If teen says, "yes," or a compromise solution is reached, this is written on a separate sheet of paper and teen and parent(s) sign their names to it. Continue in this manner, each taking a turn, until parents' three behaviors are discussed and teen's three behaviors are discussed.

Each request must be as specific as possible. Determine what changes each of you can make—negotiate and compromise where possible. *Do not agree to something you or your teen can't live with—* that will only compound the problem.

Do not discuss more than three behaviors at each contract meeting. It is important that your teen not be overwhelmed with contract sheets. What

you want for him is success at carrying out the
contract and what your teen wants from you is
that same success.

5. *Discussion of the "Do's" in Step 3.*

Step 4 may prove to be a difficult step. Feelings
may be bruised (though not intentionally). After
all, each of you have been discussing negative actions—behaviors each of you want changed. Now,
it's time to change the mood of the meeting. Toss
a coin to see who goes first. Whoever is first talk
for a few minutes about what's good about the
other person—what you like and why you like it.
Here again, you're using the list you generated at
Step 3.

When one person finishes, the other person starts.
Allow time for responses. This positive sharing
time will produce good, positive, optimistic feelings to be felt and enjoyed.

6. *Follow-up meeting.*

Decide as a group on another time to meet—a
week or two later. At that meeting discuss the
changes each of you have been making and how
well you think you're doing.

Other contract meetings can be set up when either
the parents or teen feel one is needed.

Step 4 is the difficult one—nobody likes to hear
someone else say, "I don't like it when . . ." Be careful here—self-esteem is so fragile and can be bruised
so easily. Whenever possible, use your STRAIGHT
TALK negative message skill and your ATTENTIVE
LISTENING skill when your teen starts to feel uncomfortable or uneasy.

Following is an example of a contract meeting between a father and his son.

SITUATION:

Dad and David, 13 years old, have not been getting
on well together at all. Neither one of them has a kind

thing to say about the other and their fighting and
yelling have disrupted the entire family. Dad asks
David to enter into a contract problem-solving meeting with him. David agrees.

1. *Set a meeting time.*
   Dad and David set a time and place agreeable to
   them both. Dad has paper and pencils ready when
   the meeting starts. Also, he describes for David
   what each of them will be doing throughout the
   meeting.

2. *List behaviors each wants the other to change.*
   Ten minutes only is allowed for this step. Behaviors must be specific. For example, David wants
   to put on his list: "Dad is always yelling at me."
   That's not specific enough. David needs to name
   specific times that Dad yells at him, such as,
   ". . . yells at me to put out the garbage every
   night."

David's list of behaviors that he wants his father
to change might include the following:

1. You're always yelling at me to put out the garbage every night. If you want to remind me
   that's okay—but no more yelling.
2. You expect me to do the yardwork all by myself. I need some help. I don't have all that time.
3. You're always swearing at me—you did last
   night—especially when you don't get something
   done right away.
4. You're always badmouthing my friend, George,
   and making fun of his size.
5. You treat me just like a servant—the only time
   you talk to me it's to yell at me to do something.

David looked over his list and decided to talk
about #2, #3 and #5 today.

Dad's list of behaviors that he wants David to
change might include the following:

1. You're not doing as well in school as I want
   you to.

2. You never do your chores when supposed to—such as taking out the trash and the yardwork.
3. You mouth-off all the time at your brother and sister.
4. You wear your hair too long.
5. You look dirty all the time.
6. You play the stereo so loud, I can't hear myself think.

Dad checked his list and decided to talk about #2, #3 and #6 today.

3. *List behaviors each wants the other to keep.*
   Put this list on a separate sheet of paper.
   David's list is short—he could only think of two:
   1. You try to come to all my basketball games at school.
   2. You give me $5.00 for every "A" I get on my report card.
   Dad's list was also short—he could only think of two:
   1. You're a great sportsman. I'm proud of the way you play ball.
   2. I enjoy being with you at the games and after when we stop for a bite to eat. That time together is important to me.

4. *Discussion of the "Don'ts" in Step 2.*
   David and Dad flip a coin to see who goes first. Dad wins—he goes first.

DAD: "I really get upset when the chores such as emptying the trash and the yardwork pile up because I'm afraid I'll have to do them and I've got more than I can handle already."

DAVID: (repeats what he's heard) "You really get upset when the chores such as emptying the trash and the yardwork pile up because you're afraid you'll have to do them and you've got more than you can handle already."

DAD: "Yes, that's what I said."

DAVID: "I don't see what difference it makes whether I empty the trash right after dinner or before I go to bed."

DAD: "You're feeling too much fuss is made over when you empty the trash. The important thing—and one that I've been overlooking—is that the trash does get taken care of each night."

DAVID: "That's right, Dad. It seems to me that I should be able to decide when to take out the trash without all the yelling and carrying on."

DAD: "I agree with that, David. The time the trash is emptied will be up to you. Let's put that in writing and sign it. (See contract form at end of meeting.) Now, it's your turn."

DAVID: "You expect me to do the yardwork all by myself. I need some help. I don't have all that time."

DAD: "I expect you to do the yardwork all by yourself. You need some help. You don't have all that time."

DAVID: "That's right, Dad. Saturday's my only free day—I want to spend some of that day with my friends."

DAD: "You're feeling as though you're not getting a fair shake having to do *all* the yardwork on Saturday."

DAVID: "Yeah, Dad. I think Jackie's old enough to help in the yard now—he's almost 11 years old. If he was helping me, I'd be able to finish by noon and then I could spend the afternoon with my friends."

DAD: "With Jackie to help you, the work could get done and you'd still have time for your friends, right?"

DAVSD: "Yeah, And maybe you could draw up a work sheet each week—one for me and one

for Jackie. That way we'd both know what
you wanted done on that particular Saturday."

DAD: "Great idea, David. Let's put this in writing,
too. We're making a lot of headway. Now,
it's my turn again."

DAVID: "Okay, Dad, what's next for you?"

DAD: "You mouth-off at your sister and brother
all the time and I don't like it. I don't like
hearing it and I don't like the example it sets
for them."

DAVID: "I mouth-off at my sister and brother all the
time and you don't like it. You don't like
hearing it and you don't like the example it
sets for them."

DAD: "That's right, David. I would like you to put
a little more effort into getting along with
them. I know that at times they get on your
nerves, but they do look up to you and I
know they would appreciate a little more
patience on your part, and I know I certainly
would."

DAVID: "Dad, sometimes they drive me up a wall.
They're always following me around and listening in on my phone calls—I just lose my
temper with them."

DAD: "It's really hard to have a younger brother
and sister trailing around behind you, but I
want you to consider their feelings and treat
them as you would your friends."

DAVID: "Okay, Dad, I can try. It would sure help,
though, if they tried not to follow me around
so much."

DAD: "Suppose we make your room off-limits to
them. Then when you had about all you can
take for the day, you could go to your room,
and they will know that you're not to be
bothered anymore."

DAVID: "Good idea, Dad. Let's write that one up, too."

DAD: "It's your turn again, David."

DAVID: "You're always swearing at me—you did last night—especially when I don't get something done right away."

DAD: "I'm always swearing at you—I did last night —especially when you don't get something done right away."

DAVID: "That's right, Dad. I don't like that."

DAD: "I do tend to fly off the handle, David, and I sometimes lose my temper. I'll try hard not to swear at you in the future. If I do, remind me of my promise."

DAVID: "You bet I will, Dad. Do we get to write that one up, too?"

DAD: "That's right, son. Let's see, I think it's my turn again—this is my last turn. I guess you know what my last one is going to be about— it's the stereo. You play the stereo so loud, I can't hear myself think."

DAVID: "I play the stereo so loud, you can't hear yourself think."

DAD: "That's right, David. Do you have any suggestions on how to handle this problem?"

DAVID: "Yes, Dad—how about if I get some earphones? I don't have enough money to buy them myself, but if you could loan me the money or maybe split the cost with me, that would solve the problem. Then I could use the earphones and you wouldn't even know I was listening to the stereo."

DAD: "I like that idea, David. It's worth it to me to split the cost with you, too. Let's write it up, and plan to go to the store tomorrow and pick up a set of earphones."

DAVID: "Great, Dad. Now, I have one more turn. Sometimes you treat me like a servant—the only time you talk to me it's to yell at me to do something."

DAD: "I treat you like a servant—the only time I talk to you it's to yell at you to do something."

DAVID: "That's right, Dad. You've talked more with me at this meeting than you have for the last two weeks—and you haven't yelled once."

DAD: "I really need to spend more time with you talking about things that interest us both. I get into a rut sometimes and all I can see are the chores that need doing and the things that need to be fixed, and I forget to take time to just enjoy my family. I'm going to try harder, David. Write that one up—and I'll read it every day to remind me."

DAVID: "Okay, Dad. And if you forget, I'll remind you."

5. *Discussion of the "Do's" in Step 3.*

David and Dad toss a coin again to see who goes first. Dad wins the toss again.

DAD: "I think you're a fine sportsman, David, and I want you to know how proud I am of you."

DAVID: "Gee, thanks, Dad, I didn't know you felt that way. I like the fact that you come to see me play so often. All the other kids don't have their dads rooting for them like I do."

DAD: "I wouldn't miss one of your games if I could help it, David. And anyhow it gives me some time to be out with you alone when we stop for something to eat on the way home. I enjoy those times."

DAVID: "I do, too, Dad. I also like it when you give me $5 for every "A" I get—I wish I got more "A's"."

6. *Follow-up meeting.*

DAD: "Let's meet again in two weeks and see how we're doing—what do you say?"

DAVID: "Okay, Dad."

Whether you choose the family meeting problem-solving process or the contract meeting problem-solving process is up to you. Both work.

The following Journal Exercise will give you an opportunity to determine what battle you want to fight. Choose your battles carefully. Fight only the important ones—the lesser ones may then disappear or at least diminish in intensity.

JOURNAL EXERCISE #14

In your Journal list ten things about your teen that bother you the most. Choose the top three that you would really like to do something about.

Decide which problem-solving process you want to use. If it's the family meeting, pick one topic from your top three choices. If it's the contract meeting, use all three of your top choices.

Write out the specific situation(s). Compose STRAIGHT TALK negative message(s). Set a time for your meeting with your teen. Write out the outcome.

1. List ten things.
2. Choose top three.
3. Decide which meeting you will hold.
4. Write out situation(s).
5. Compose STRAIGHT TALK negative message(s).
6. Put Step 1 into action.
7. Write out the outcome of the meeting.

(Sample)   **CONTRACT**
between
Dad _____ (name of parent or teen)
David _____ (name of teen or parent)

SUBJECT:
(a separate contract sheet for each subject).
Date _____ Signed:

_____
Dad

_____
David

CHAPTER 10

Authority/Control

Authority can be positive when it means influence, permission, responsibility; and control is usually negative when it means regulate, restrain, direct or manipulate. If a teen were asked what he thinks is lacking most of his life, the most frequent answer would be, "I feel helpless—everybody runs my life but me!"—which indicates a need for more freedom in and responsibility for his life.

Great teachers strive to influence their students and parents should strive for this same goal. Control over a child lasts only until that child is bigger than you are—influence over a child can last your lifetime, your child's lifetime and your grandchild's lifetime.

When children are small we use both our authority and our control—our authority when we influence behavior and our control in areas affecting our children's health, safety and welfare. As our children grow older and bigger control needs to be lessened. You need to use more authority/influence. You need to trust that your teen can learn to make his own decisions—whether they are right or wrong. Make suggestions, ask questions, point out inconsistencies—be the influencer but allow your teen the right to make his own decisions.

The indiscriminate use of control by parents on teens forces those teens to seek ways of deflecting such control or restraint.

How did you react?

Think back to your teenage years. How did you respond when your parent used control on you? Did you retaliate with aggressive behavior? Did you lie? Did you cheat? Did you run away? Did you do what you were ordered to do and then take out your frustration and anger on a younger brother or sister? Did you hate your parent for using control?

We all react in some way to being surrounded by control and restraints. When a parent uses control constantly, he is robbing his child of the knowledge and experience of influence, justice, compassion, trust in another's capabilities, and respect for other people. This parent is also robbing him of the opportunity to learn to trust his own experience and judgment.

Authority and control are important. They are a part of living. And, they also have a place in your household. There are appropriate uses of authority and control. The trouble is that control is hard to turn off. The more we use it, the more we want to use it. It's like eating peanuts—once you start, it's hard to stop!

When children are babies, we use control frequently. "Take the cat's paw out of your mouth!" "Don't put your fingers in the socket!" "It's time to put away your toys." "Eat your vegetables." "Don't disturb Daddy's papers." And so on. BUT, almost without exception, when we said any of the above, we said it, not only with care and concern, but also we tagged on some reason or explanation for the statement. The youngster to whom we spoke these orders or commands almost always felt loved, cared for and respected.

Because control is so easy to use, we are tempted

to use it more often than we intend. As our children grow up, instead of using less control and becoming more and more the influencer or teacher, we find ourselves hooked on using control, restraints and manipulation. It takes less of our time, and time being the great commodity it is today, we can rationalize our use of control. But now something happens to the way we use control. We no longer come across to our teens as caring or loving. We don't tolerate their questions—their eternal "whys?" It's not quite as easy now as it was when they were youngsters but still we find ourselves trapped in our control rut. It takes some skills to build a ladder out of that rut. Our parents, for the most part, didn't know these skills— so here we are, one more generation falling back on what we know—knowing it doesn't work even as we use it, but not really sure what else to do.

Slowly, parents are becoming aware of the things they don't know. And many of them are learning new ways of parenting either through books such as this one or by attending classes at the Institutes for Adolescent Studies across the country, or through parenting classes at their churches or community colleges.

If we find ourselves in the control trap and want to get out, how do we start? First, you need to be aware of the times you use your control. The following Journal Exercise will help you pinpoint those times.

JOURNAL EXERCISE #15

In your Journal, make a list of the times you ordered or commanded your teen to do something this past week. Categorize your list. How many concerned household chores? How many concerned household rules? How many concerned school work? Add other categories as you need them.

Look over each item in each category and determine whether or not you could have han-

dled the item in question any other way, such
as by sending a STRAIGHT TALK message or
initiating a family meeting or a contract meeting.

Compose a Straight Talk negative message
for each item. Send your messages the next
time these situations arise.

1. List the times you ordered or commanded
   your teen this past week.
2. Put these commands and orders into categories.
3. Compose STRAIGHT TALK negative
   messages for each item.
4. Send these messages the next time the
   situation arises.

Each parent has a unique parenting style. Some of
you may find that you need to continue to use control
statements (orders and commands). When you do,
stick to the issue at hand, make your statements strong,
but not judgmental, and keep them free of put-downs.
Then shift gears and use your ATTENTIVE LISTEN-
ING skill.

Your teen won't like your statement any more than
he would have before, but he will feel cared for and
respected when you are willing to listen to what he
has to say in response to it. Weigh what your teen
has to say—he may be saying what you wanted to say
to your father, but didn't dare. In other words, respect
and value your teen as a person worthy of your time
and attention. Remember, you are now modeling for
him a positive use of control. The way you handle
yourself in this situation is the way your teen will
handle himself when his time comes.

Some of you may find that you want to use control
less and less. When you find yourself wanting to make
a control statement, change that statement to a
STRAIGHT TALK message. When you've sent your

STRAIGHT TALK mesage, shift gears and use your ATTENTIVE LISTENING skill. You, too, are now modeling an even more positive use of authority and control, but here you are tempering its use with compassion. That's an unbeatable combination!

Following are two examples of parenting styles. Example #1 shows a parenting style that includes control statements. Example #2 shows a parenting style that does not include control statements.

EXAMPLE #1:
Situation:

Mary, age 15, has just received a telephone call from Bill, age 17, inviting her to a rock concert being held in a city which is an hour's ride away from home.

MARY: "Mom, guess what? Bill just called and invited me to go to hear the group I've been telling you about. Everything's all arranged. Mom, can I go? Please say 'yes'!"

MOM: "I don't know, Mary, we'll discuss it when your father gets home."

MARY: "Oh, Mom, if you're going to ask Dad, I'll never be able to go."

(later that evening)

"Hi, Dad, guess what? Bill called me today and invited me to go with him to that rock concert I was telling you about."

DAD: "Now, Honey, you know how I feel about those concerts. Bill is a senior and it's all right for him to go, but you're only a sophomore. You'll have plenty of time for that sort of thing." (Control Statement)

MARY: "Does that mean 'No'?"

DAD: "I'm afraid it does, Honey."

MARY: "I never get to do anything! You treat me like a baby! I hate it here!"

DAD: "You're really feeling disappointed—you had your heart set on this, didn't you." (A-L)

MARY: "Yes, I did. Now I'll be the laughing stock of

the school when everyone finds out why I can't
go! Oh, Dad, why can't I go? Nothing will
happen."

DAD: "I trust you, Mary, really I do. It's just hard
for me to realize that you're growing up so fast.
I'll work at it harder, but it's going to take
time."

MARY: "And what am I supposed to do in the meantime? Hibernate?"

DAD: "I'm sorry, Mary, truly I am. But, the answer
is 'No' at least for this time."

Mary is bound to feel some resentment toward her
Dad, but she has an understanding of the reasons
behind her Dad's "No." She'll find a way to handle
her disappointment as well as a way to handle any
flack she may get from her school friends. She, also,
and this is more important, understands her father a
little better each time he reveals his reasons or criteria
for his "Yes" or "No." She sees him as trying to come
to grips with the changing times. If she thinks there
is some hope for change, she will probably feel free
to bring up the subject again. In other words, she
can exist until she's feeling better about the situation,
which will probably be when the concert date has
come and gone.

Her Dad has expressed his concern that she's growing up so fast—and what father hasn't expressed (or
at least felt) that concern? That disclosure makes him
more human to Mary and in the weeks to come she
may tease him about that statement.

Dad's statement, "You're really feeling disappointed
—you had your heart set on this, didn't you," incor-
porated his ATTENTIVE LISTENING skill. If the
interchange between him and Mary had ended with
Mary saying, ". . . I hate it here!" there would probably have been a break in communication between
father and daughter that might take weeks to mend.
If enough of these breaks happen, there just isn't

enough time between breaks for the mending to take place.

EXAMPLE #2:
Situation:

Mary, age 15, has just received a telephone call from Bill, age 17, inviting her to a rock concert being held in a city which is an hour's ride away from home.

MARY: "Mom, guess what? Bill just called and invited me to go to hear the group I've been telling you about. Everything's all arranged. Mom, can I go? Please say 'Yes'!"

MOM: "I'm not sure, Mary. Your father, you, and I need to sit down together and discuss some things before we can give you an answer. This is a first for you, Honey, and I know how excited you must be."

MARY: "Oh, Mom, I really want to go to this concert. Did you know that it's been sold out for weeks?"

MOM: "Of course, I know—you've been talking about it for weeks! Well, we'll get things settled tonight when Dad comes home. In the meantime, why don't you find out who else is going, how you're going to get there and how long you'll be gone. We'll need that information."

MARY: "Okay, Mom, I'll call and find out. (worried) I hope Dad lets me go, you know how he can't stand rock music."

MOM: "I know, Honey. Get your information together and we'll talk more tonight."
(later that evening)

MARY: "Hi, Dad, guess what? Bill called me today and invited me to go with him to that rock concert I was telling you about."

DAD: "You're feeling pretty excited about this rock concert." (A-L)

MARY: "Oh, Dad, say I can go—it's the best thing that's ever happened to me."

DAD: "When I read about the things that happen at these concerts, I can't believe it. I knew that one day soon you would want to go. I am frightened to think of you and Bill there alone when heaven knows what could happen." (S-T message)

MARY: "But, Dad, I'm fifteen and Bill's seventeen—what could happen that we couldn't take care of?"

DAD: "You're feeling you could take care of anything, Honey, but I still see you as the baby of the family." (A-L and S-T)

MARY: "Oh, Dad, I'll probably be the 'baby of the family' for the rest of my life! Let me tell you more about the evening, Dad, then maybe you'll be able to see that I'll be all right."

DAD: "Okay, Honey, let's talk more about the evening and maybe we can find an acceptable solution for both of us. How about you, mom and me getting together right after dinner?"

MARY: "Great, Dad—we'll talk more then."

Dad sent his STRAIGHT TALK message, and then he shifted gears and used his ATTENTIVE LISTENING skill. Mary has had an opportunity to express excitement, enthusiasm and hope—and Dad recognized her feelings and was careful not to step on them.

It may be that Mary will be allowed to go to the rock concert. Dad may find that Bill's older brother and his date are going and will be driving, or Mary may know of another couple who are in their 20's who can pick them up after the concert. There are many alternatives that will be generated during the problem-solving meeting. It may resolve itself with a creative solution or the solution may be a negotiated one.

Whatever the outcome, Mary and her Dad will

benefit from the positive interaction which will result in greater feelings of self-esteem for each of them. The bond between them will also become stronger. Mary will be more likely to seek out her Father when she has a problem because she knows he will listen. If they talk enough about music, Dad may even become a "fan" of Mary's favorite rock group! When you start to "like" your teenagers, you find you also start liking some of the things they like. Turnabout is fair play and soon your teens begin to like one or two—maybe more—things about you and the things you like.

Authority and control play important roles in our lives. These roles can be positive ones. They only become negative roles when we abuse them.

CHAPTER 11

Anger

This chapter on anger is divided into three sections: General Background, the Angry Parent and the Angry Adolescent. This first section deals with anger as a general subject and gives you the background you will need to understand your anger and your teen's anger.

1. GENERAL BACKGROUND

Anger is a necessary, productive and healthy feeling.

Our problem in the past has been that we tried to stifle angry feelings or we dealt with these feelings in ways that were destructive and/or counterproductive.

When feelings of anger are constantly stifled, both physical and mental health deteriorate. Anger is an energy that must find some outlet. If we deny ourselves that outlet, this same energy starts to consume us. If we allow ourselves to express these angry feelings inappropriately—in a destructive or counterproductive way—we are left with the additional problems of guilt and bits and pieces of relationships which could not weather a destructive release of anger.

We live in a complicated, complex, industrialized society, and there are a lot of situations both inside and outside our family that make us angry each day.

A person who is dealing with his anger in a constructive way will usually admit to getting angry anywhere from three to five times a day. A person who says, "I never get angry," is not being honest with himself nor is he in touch with his feelings. If you stuff your anger back inside, your anger will turn on you and make itself felt in other ways. In extreme cases, for some people, anger turned inward results in depression —the single most common mental problem—and for others, anger turned inward can result in suicide. This same anger turned inward can result in a host of physical illnesses and diseases, often largely psychological, such as high blood pressure, stress, heart attacks, ulcers, colitis, acne, psoriasis, backaches, headaches, cancer, etc.

Picture anger as a big ball of fire. When you're angry, that big ball of fire is sitting inside you. If it doesn't get released in some way, that ball of fire stays with you, and as we keep stuffing ourselves with more and more balls of fire, we are bound to experience the consequences in one or more of the ways mentioned above.

Most of us don't know how to release our anger constructively, so we find ourselves in a terrible bind. If we release our anger by name-calling, or yelling at people when they're not at fault, we are attacking and hurting other people; and if we don't release it, but keep stuffing ourselves with anger fireballs, we are endangering our own mental and physical health.

DESTRUCTIVE, COUNTERPRODUCTIVE WAYS
OF HANDLING ANGER:

We usually handle our anger in one of three ways —all of which are destructive and counterproductive:
1. *We displace our anger inappropriately.*
   Someone makes us angry and there we sit with that fireball inside us. We are unwilling or unable to

confront the person who made us angry so we hold our anger inside. Later, we dump our anger on someone else.

For example: John's supervisor has called him into a department meeting. When John enters the meeting room, his supervisor tells John that the figures John gave him were not correct. John is blamed for the inaccurate report. John knows that the figures he used for the report were given to him by his supervisor, but he can't bring himself to say anything at the meeting because he's afraid his supervisor will place his job on the line. John leaves the meeting consumed with anger. That fireball of anger sits inside John until he goes home. As soon as he walks in the front door, he explodes—he yells at his wife because the house is not clean, he yells at his son because the yard doesn't look right, he yells at his daughter because she's wearing a certain outfit. The family is stunned—the house is as clean as it always is, the yardwork is up to date and his daughter's outfit is fine. John was discharging his anger indiscriminately and in the process has hurt his wife, his son and his daughter. When John starts yelling, the fireball of anger inside him slowly dies, but now he has to mend the damage he's done at home and he still has to face the situation at the office tomorrow.

2. *We suppress our anger.*

We recognize that we are angry (conscious behavior), but we are unwilling or unable to take care of those anger feelings at the time. In the example above, John suppressed his anger at the office —he was afraid that he would lose his job, so he made a decision not to confront his supervisor. He then went home and *displaced* his anger, not caring for the moment where he sent those feelings of anger—wanting only to put out the flames of that fireball!

3. *We repress our anger.*

We don't even admit that we are angry (unconscious behavior). People who repress anger are often afraid to admit to having any angry feelings. They were brought up to believe that "nice" people never get angry. These people cheat themselves by not getting angry, If they are afraid to feel anger, they may also be afraid to feel love, or joy, or happiness. We can't bury feelings selectively—if we bury anger, we will usually bury other feelings and emotions.

If we suppress our anger enough times and just keeping stuffing it down inside, we need to remember that it has to go somewhere—if not outward, then inward. If we repress our anger—not even recognizing that we are angry, that fireball still needs someplace to go—and it will find a home somewhere in *us*.

In learning about anger, it is crucial to understand that you must separate actions of anger from the feelings of anger. There is absolutely nothing wrong in your feeling angry and there is nothing wrong with thinking about whatever you'd like to do with that feeling.

Very often it is inappropriate to carry out the action that comes to mind with the feelings, but remember that no matter how violent your thoughts, it's OKAY to have your THOUGHTS. It is NOT OKAY to carry out the ACTIONS.

For example, Dad returns from a business trip to find that his 17-year-old son has used his workshop in the garage, without permission, to fix his automobile. Not only did his son not clean up the workshop and put away the tools, but three of the tools are totally ruined. Dad feels so angry at that moment he would like to strangle his son. Then almost immediately he feels that he shouldn't be so angry and that he should try to control his anger.

Feeling the anger is healthy, normal and appropriate. Feeling so strongly *for a while* that he'd like to strangle his son is also normal and appropriate. Often we allow ourselves to feel too guilty about thoughts. Of course, it is important that he NOT strangle his son, but it is also important that he allow himself to feel his anger.

Let's take another example: a woman is driving on the freeway and suddenly a car swerves into her lane of traffic and only by slamming on her brakes and skidding for a couple of hundred feet is she able to avoid a serious accident. Right at that moment, she feels so angry at the driver of the other car she would like to ram her car into his. Again, there is absolutely nothing wrong with feeling that amount or intensity of anger—it is normal, appropriate and healthy. What *would* be wrong would be to ram her car into the other driver's car.

Experience your angry feelings with as much intensity as you want, and allow yourself an action-thought (such as strangling your son or ramming the other driver's car) to fit your feeling—but don't act out or feel guilty about those action-thoughts.

Constructive Ways of Handling Anger

We encourage you to express your anger when you're feeling it wherever you can: work relationships (if you have that type of environment where this is possible), social relationships, and most especially family relationships with all members of your family.

*Understanding your anger and expressing it in a
healthy manner is crucial to your relationship
with your teenager. It is important that you provide a role model showing him how to handle
anger and it is important that you and your teen
have a healthy give and take relationship between
you.*

When dealing with anger, ask yourself four questions:
1. What am I feeling? Is it anger—if it is, recognize
   it as such.
2. Where is my anger coming from? Identify the
   source of your anger. Is somebody stepping on my
   foot? Is it my boss who is making me angry?
3. Why is what's happening making me angry? Once
   the source is identified, the "why" will be answered.
   Is somebody stepping on my foot? Yes, I'm angry
   because it hurts! Is my boss making me angry?
   Yes, I'm angry because I feel helpless in this situation.
4. How can I deal with my anger?
   A. TALK WITH THE PERSON WHO IS MAK-
   ING YOU ANGRY (IF YOU FEEL YOU CAN)
   AND SEND HIM A STRAIGHT TALK MES-
   SAGE ABOUT YOUR ANGER. Remember, then,
   to shift gears and use your ATTENTIVE LISTEN-
   ING skill.
   B. GET SOMEONE TO LISTEN TO YOU TALK
   ABOUT YOUR ANGER. This will help put out
   that ball of fire sitting there inside you.
   C. WORK IT OFF IN SOME WAY. Play tennis,
   hit pillows, jog, run, etc. Let that energy work its
   way out.
   The first method above—talking with the person
who has made you angry—is by far the best one. By
confronting the person who has made you angry, and

talking to him, you are able to bring down your emotional temperature just about all the way. As you talk out what's made you angry, both of you get to know each other a little better—your relationship is strengthened. Confrontation doesn't have to be hostile or sadistic.

The second and third methods above may leave some anger feelings unresolved. It certainly helps for the time being to have someone listen to you while you ventilate your feelings of anger, but that anger may again rise to the surface in a day or two, and once again will need an outlet. The same is true for working anger off—it certainly helps, but the anger may reappear in a day or two and, again, you will have to handle it in one or more of the ways mentioned above.

2. Angry Adolescent

The normal adolescent is filled with anger and rage much of the time. He will frequently react to a situation with far more intense and longer-lasting anger than the situation warrants.

The over-reaction helps the teen release some of the stored-up anger, and frustration, confusion, and helplessness that growing up in any industrialized society produces.

It's hard for parents to live with an angry teenager because he is sometimes very difficult to be around. And to live with him and continue to nurture him during this period of growth from childhood to adulthood can be downright impossible at times.

As a parent you don't have to like these expressions of anger, but you do need to understand and accept that your teen needs to express his anger and rage. Your teenager, who may often be irrational, who may fly off the handle without provocation and who probably is a pain-in-the-neck most of the time, needs to know that he has the room and the space to express his anger, and hopefully, some help from his parents on how to deal with this anger and rage constructively.

The best way to release anger—both for teens and parents—is to talk directly to the person who is the cause of your anger. Occasionally, this is possible for the teenager, especially when his angry feelings are directed at family members, his friends and some of the people he encounters in his daily life. In many cases, because of the situation, he will be unable to confront these people directly.

For example, if you son's girlfriend has broken up with him and doesn't want to see him anymore, your son may find it difficult or impossible to talk to her about the anger he's feeling. A teen who has a part-time job may get angry at his boss, but he may feel that if he confronts his boss, he'll be fired.

As a parent you can help your teen disperse the hurt he's feeling by encouraging him to talk about what's making him angry. You now have at your command your ATTENTIVE LISTENING skill which can help your teen ventilate his felings of anger and frustration. In addition to reducing your teen's emotional temperature, you are being a role model which he in turn will use both with his friends and when he's a parent of a teenager.

3. ANGRY PARENT

Most parents of teens can find literally dozens of things they are unhappy about that their teen does. Sometimes, unknowingly, many parents also are waging almost continual warfare with their adolescents by hesitating to tell their teens all the things they (the teens) are doing wrong. The teen, on the other hand, feels that he's constantly being yelled at and criticized. He feels anger and parents feel anger.

Often a parent will get angry because his teen is

wearing his hair too long, or his room is dirty, etc., and before you know it an out-and-out battle erupts between the teen and his parent. A parent may get his teen to clean up his room for a short time or to cut his hair shorter, but in the process both parent and teen feel that they are continually at war. You may "win the battle" over a specific issue, but lose the war in terms of creating an atmosphere of good feelings and good communication at home.

Keep in mind that if your adolescent is progressing normally, he's going to be very difficult and almost impossible a good part of the time! If you're tempted to say, "I give up!" or "I don't care anymore!" or "It's gotten so I hate my son!," remember that rebelling, being difficult goes with the territory of adolescence.

We are not saying that you shouldn't "do battle" with your teen—what we are saying is "choose your battles carefully." Don't make your home the scene of too many insignificant battles—if it's a battlefield, it cannot be the place of refuge and nurturing it should be.

Your STRAIGHT TALK messages will help you handle your angry feelings, your ATTENTIVE LISTENING skill will help you reduce angry feelings that other family members may have, and your PROBLEM-SOLVING skills will help you resolve difficulties that are producing angry feelings.

The following Journal Exercise will help you become aware of your anger and give you practice in composing appropriate STRAIGHT TALK messages to handle those feelings.

JOURNAL EXERCISE #16
In your Journal briefly describe the times you were angry this week. Write after each situation how you resolved your feelings of anger. Compose a STRAIGHT TALK message for

each situation. If appropriate, send your message to the person who made you angry.
1. Briefly describe situations which made you feel angry.
2. Tell how you resolved each situation.
3. Compose STRAIGHT TALK messages for each situation.
4. If appropriate, send your STRAIGHT TALK messages.

CHAPTER 12

The Single Parent and the Working Mother

Today, because of necessity and/or fulfillment, more and more families have a working mother or a single parent in the household. Add to that adolescents, or an adolescent and other children, and problems can multiply and escalate rapidly.

THE SINGLE PARENT

Difficult as it can be to raise a teenager with two parents, the single parent almost always has even more problems. A single parent is usually a mother, but gradually more fathers are joining the ranks of the single parent.

A typical day in the life of a single parent starts out early in the morning when she gets up, gets dressed, cooks breakfast, eats breakfast (if she has time), packs lunches, gets the kids up, makes sure they have something to eat, gets them out to the bus or the carpool with books and lunch sacks in tow. Next, she puts the milk and butter back into the refrigerator, and stacks the breakfast dishes—there is rarely time to wash them or to make beds or to pick up the living room. She rushes to her car or to the corner to catch the bus, hoping that traffic is light so she can arrive at work on time.

She works hard all day. She may even have had an urgent call from school which she handled as well as she could on the phone, but probably worried about it all afternoon. Now at last, the work day is over and she can start for home. Out she goes to face the rush hour traffic—first stopping at the market to pick up an item or two missed during her weekly shopping. And, finally, she's home. Home to a house that still has the breakfast dishes in the sink, beds unmade and a messy living room. Where to start first?

But, before she can do anything, she remembers the phone call from school. First things first, she tackles the school problem with her teen. When that's taken care of, one of the other children needs her.

It's 7 p.m. now and she's just starting supper. One of the teens has the stereo on as high as it will go. The youngest child is yelling at him to lower it so she can hear her favorite television program. She finally gets dinner on the table and if she's lucky, has the kitchen clean and the living room picked up by 9 p.m. The kids had homework, so she got no help there. The beds? Why make them? It's time to go to bed again!

When the house finally quiets down, Mom realizes that she didn't get the rent check in the mail. She meant to ask Jimmy to mail the check after dinner and then forgot. The garbage didn't get out tonight either. Jimmy was supposed to do it, but hasn't been keeping up with his chores lately. She must remember to talk to him about that tomorrow. Now that she finally has a chance to sit down, all she can think of is, "When will this all end? When will there be time for me? Will there ever be time enough for the kids? Is my life over?"

Soon, after everyone is in bed, she collapses into bed herself. This day is repeated five times a week. And now the weekend is here. She can barely struggle through the chores of cleaning, washing, shopping, ad infinitum. She has no spouse to turn to for support and comfort. No one to turn to—no one to complain to, no one with whom to share the load, no one with whom to plan for the future.

This goes on seven days a week, year after year. Add to their frustration and fatigue the fact that most single parents also have financial problems—it's no wonder they sometimes ask themselves: Where does it all end?

> *Being a single parent is simply an incredibly difficult job and it is almost a miracle that single parents are able to make it at all.*

All of the feelings that two-parent families have toward their teenagers are usually experienced in a much deeper way by the single parent. The load is greater for the single parent. In addition to the frustration, the anger, and the rage that a single parent feels, she typically has other feelings, such as:

"I would really like to get rid of this kid!"

"I wish I never had any children."

"I wish they would go to live with their father (or mother) and never come back!"

"I feel like giving up!"

"It isn't fair!"

When two-parent families have these feelings, and they do, they have each other to talk things out with; they have each other for support; they can laugh about it together, they can plan for the future together.

When the single parent has these feelings—and if she doesn't, something's wrong—she's alone; she may find it difficult to discuss these feelings with a friend or another family member.

These thoughts and feelings are perfectly normal, natural and typical. In Chapter 11 when we discussed anger, we said it's all right to have these feelings and you shouldn't feel guilty about having them. As long as they remain only feelings they are appropriate and perfectly normal. The inappropriate or abnormal behavior occurs when these thoughts and feelings are translated into actions.

Very often single parents will feel guilty because they think they're not doing enough for their kids, or that they're not doing things well enough. Guilt piles on guilt and underneath that guilt hides anger!

Acknowledge your right to feel these feelings and your anger. You're right! Life isn't fair. Your mental health will improve greatly if you can acknowledge the injustice and the unfairness in your life.

Another problem a single parent encounters is the lack of a support system. The single parent needs to know that she's not the only person to experience this lack of support. Try to find people and groups with whom to share similar experiences. Your church may have a single parent group or your community may sponsor such a group.

We believe that for your kids to be happy, you have to be happy. Try to take some time for yourself each week. Try to find people who share some of the same experiences you do. Try to become each other's support system. The better you feel about yourself, the better parent you can be to your children. They in turn become easier to live with because they start to feel better about themselves.

The Journal Exercises at the end of this chapter were designed especially for the single parent and the working mother. Do them now before you go to the next chapter.

THE WORKING MOTHER

There are today 16.2 million working mothers in America. The working mother frequently has two fulltime jobs. One away from home—the job for which she gets paid; and one at home, running the household.

She is a lucky woman, indeed, if she has a husband who shoulders his share of the household and family responsibility.

If she doesn't, she soon starts to experience the same feelings a single parent has. She may even wonder if a single parent hasn't an easier time of it! At least she—the single parent—doesn't expect support from her spouse, who is no longer in the home, so her disappointment at this lack of support is not as acute as the working mother's disappointment. The latter experiences this hurt, disappointment, anger, and ultimately guilt, time and time again. And each time it happens it diminishes her feelings of self-worth and self-confidence. She may begin to see herself as a slave to her family and when that happens, as time goes on, her family may increasingly treat her as one.

Not only does she work very hard at her job (which she may or may not enjoy), but she comes home to a family who may still rely on her to do everything— the washing, the ironing, the beds, the dishes, fix dinner, shop, pick up after them, ad nauseum.

Before long, the working mother feels unloved, unappreciated, and sometimes unable to cope—to handle her life. She finds herself thinking the same thoughts a single parent thinks:

"I would really like to just run away someplace— anyplace."

"How long will it be before the kids are gone?"

"If I had it to do over again, I would never have gotten married."

"I wish we never had any kids!"

If she has a sensitive, sympathetic husband, she soon finds herself sharing these sentiments and talking out ways to put everything back on the track again. A problem shared somehow doesn't seem to be so insurmountable.

If she doesn't have a husband she can share things with, then she must do the same things a single parent needs to do: find people who share the same experiences. Give each other the support each of you needs. In this case, the better you feel about yourself, the better parent and wife you can be. As you feel better about yourself, you project a different image to your spouse and your children—and they react differently to you. You also feel more confident about letting your family know what you expect from them and what they can expect from you in the future.

Once you have a support group (see the Journal Exercise below), you can better utilize the skills in this book as individual situations or problems arise.

JOURNAL EXERCISE #17

In your Journal make a list of the things you did this week for your kids. Then make a list of the things you did this week for *you*. Which is longer?

Do something special for *you* this coming week. Decide what that special something will be. Write it down in your Journal right now. Are you going for a walk, out to dinner, to visit a friend, go bowling? When you've done what you promised yourself, check it off.

Now, list two things you will do for you between now and next week. In the beginning you may have to force yourself to take care of you. It gets easier when you see how much more relaxed and happier your family is—and it's all because you are feeling more relaxed and happier. Don't let a week go by that you haven't done at least two things for you. Note in your Journal what they are and check them off as you complete them. Once this becomes a habit, you don't need to make this entry each week.

JOURNAL EXERCISE #18

Title a page in your Journal, "My Support System."

1. List the people you can go to for support and encouragement, such as family members, friends, people at work, neighbors.
2. Put a check mark by those people you've confided in during the last week.
3. Do you have at least four people on your list? If not, try to add to your list until you have at least four people you can call on for support. Before you add a person's name to your list, discuss an issue or two with him. If you still feel good about that person, add his name to your list.
4. Make it a point to talk or visit at least once each week with one of the people on your list. Keep your list current and active.

CHAPTER 13

Tips for Parents

This chapter includes a variety of subjects that we think should be included in a book about teenagers. Many of these subject areas are complex enough to have an entire book devoted to them. For now, along with the skills included in this book, we want to add the following tips which we hope will sharpen your view of adolescence.

LETTING GO

Kahlil Gibran, in his beautiful book, *The Prophet*, wrote:

Your children are not your children.
They are the sons and daughters of Life's longing for itself.
They come through you but not from you.
And though they are with you yet they belong not to you.

From the day he's born a child works his way to adulthood, and along the way, parents have to know when to let go, when to allow the youngster the freedom to take the next step by himself. That's hard. But when you finish this book and have at your command the communication skills and the background you need to relate to your teen, and you can see how your teen is accepting more and more responsibility, learning more and more of decision-making, understanding how to seek alternatives, and making choices based on those alternatives—then maybe you will feel easier about the letting-go process.

A child of three needs to experience the sense of accomplishment that comes from knowing he did a job all by himself and that he did the job well. A parent has to allow his three-year-old the freedom to do a job (after the skill has been taught) and the parent has the responsibility as well to let the child know it was a job well done. If a child of three needs this sense of accomplishment, how much more important must it be to a teenager, who mainly because of his age, is beset by doubts every day.

Responsibility is learned just as skills are learned. We become responsible by doing, by trying— each attempt is a brick in our road to independence. Whether that road is laid with bricks of success or potholes of failure depends in large part on parents.

Opportunities for teens to do things on their own need to be provided by parents. Allowing our teens the space and freedom to make their own mistakes, to try out new ways, to march to the tune of their own drummers, is hard to do.

Letting go may be more difficult for some parents than for others. Frequently, mothers who devote their whole lives to their children, always doing everything for them, sometimes smothering them in an effort to keep them close to home, find that when the kids finally do leave home, they experience the "empty nest syndrome." This mother may believe she no longer has any identity or value as a person, since both her identity and her value were based on her role as a mother.

Don't hang on to your children—allow them to grow up—allow them to be normal teenagers.

From the moment your child is born, you should be

preparing him to be on his own. Only then will he be able to live a full, happy, responsible life, satisfying to himself and to the world around him. If you can do this, when your child reaches adulthood and goes out on his own, the loss you're bound to feel will be tempered with acceptance, a sense of accomplishment and a feeling of relief. Life continues. Parenthood is only a segment—a very important segment—of a full, well-lived life.

WORRY

Parents often find that during their youngster's teenage years they worry like they've never worried before! As your teen gets older and is assuming more responsibility and earning more privileges such as staying out later at night, there is often more cause to worry. Today, parents worry about their teen's driving a car, being exposed to drugs, alcohol, and members of the opposite sex, for example—all of which teens encounter as a normal part of their day-to-day living.

Parents spend an enormous amount of time worrying—worrying is something most parents do very well. But it's also a natural characteristic of parents who love and care for their teens. But frequently that worry turns to anger. A parent, waiting up for his teen to come home because it's well past curfew time, will likely spend that time worrying. However, when the teen gets home, the worry turns to anger, and this parent may often shout, yell, and scream at his teen. As we discussed in detail in our anger chapter (Chapter 11), as well as our STRAIGHT TALK chapter (Chapter 5), these feelings of anger need to be expressed and talked out, otherwise communication in the home can come to a standstill.

If you are a worrier, here are five things for you to be aware of:

1. Know that almost all concerned parents worry.

2. When your teen has caused you undue worry (as in the example above) and you have feelings you want to express, be sure to send a STRAIGHT TALK message.

3. Say to yourself again and again, "worrying is my problem," and try not to take it out on your teen.

4. Be aware that excess worrying may be upsetting you. Try to do something else . . . read a book, watch television, talk to your spouse, go to bed.

5. Remember: It is very rare that something really bad happens and that most of your worrying is for nothing.

Parent in the Middle

Most of the time the parent in the middle is the mother. However, sometimes it can be the father. The parent in the middle becomes the buffer between the adolescent and the other parent. It's a miserable experience for the person in the middle. That person feels torn between two people she loves and feels that these two people are destroying each other.

Worse than that, the person in the middle may feel that she has to choose between the two people involved. This produces feelings of anger and resentment. She feels torn—if she takes the side of her spouse, the child feels totally alone, isolated and his problems will increase. If she takes the side of their child, the spouse will feel betrayed and angry.

We feel unequivocally that, for the mental health of your teenager, it is important that you support him when you feel he's right. If you think your teen has a point, he should be heard, he needs your support and you need to give him that support. If you don't, that omission will contribute heavily to your teen's feelings of worthlessness and lack of self-esteem. If you think your teen is right, and your spouse is wrong, it is imperative that you support your adolescent.

There are several ways you can express your support of your teen. One way is shown in the example below.

When Tom got angry at his teenage son, Jack, he would lose his temper and say, "I hate you, you bastard. I wish you had never been born." When this happened, Jack's mother, Janet would say to Tom, "Don't say that." In private she would tell Tom not to say things like that, but Jack never knew this. Jack assumed that his mother agreed with his father, and that she also wished he were never born. He felt that his mother simply didn't want her husband to SAY it—although Jack felt that both his parents felt it. Unfortunately, an assumption like that is very logical for a teen to make. Obviously, every time Jack's father did this, Jack's self-esteem and self-acceptance were damaged.

Other ways that Janet could have supported Jack would be for her to say directly to Tom (with Jack present), "I don't agree with that and I wish you wouldn't say it." Or, if she couldn't say that to her husband in front of Jack, later to Jack alone she might say, "You know I love you and I'm very glad you're my son. I don't feel the way your father does and he probably doesn't feel that way either, except when he's angry. It's important to me that you know how I feel."

A parent in the middle doesn't have to stay there. Try to get your spouse to use this book and the skills in it. If you use the skills and approach your spouse in a non-judgmental way, your chances of getting him to try these new communication skills are greatly enhanced. The example below shows how one parent in the middle refused to stay there, what he did about it, and how he helped his wife work with him and not against him.

Arthur and Joyce could not accept their 15-year-old son, Tim, using marijuana. They were totally against it, believing it was wrong, that it was harmful to him and disrespectful to them. As their son increased his use of marijuana, they found themselves becoming alienated from him. There were more and more fights and arguments within the family. Joyce kept telling her husband that she wanted to disown Tim, that she wanted to run away. What she finally did was stop speaking to Tim. Arthur thought that he was in the middle and he didn't think the situation was getting any better. As a matter of fact, the situation between his son, his wife and himself was deteriorating frighteningly fast. Arthur was able to let Tim know that he still cared about him. He realized that he couldn't stop his son from using marijuana despite the fact that he disapproved of it. But he showed his son, by spending time with him, talking and listening to him, that he still loved him, cared for him and wanted very much to be his father. By doing this, Arthur was giving Tim the support he needed and Tim's self-esteem and feeling of self-worth improved greatly.

Joyce, on the other hand, was unable to do what Arthur did and as a result she shut herself off from the family and had very little to do with Tim. She gained weight and started having bouts of depression. At this point, Arthur told her of his concern for her and how what was happening was threatening the very foundations of the family. He asked her to try to do some of the things that he was doing—to try using the skills outlined in this book. She felt Arthur's love and concern and tried—and succeeded—using her new skills. It didn't happen overnight, but eventually, as Tim was able to feel good about himself and where he fit into the family, his use of marijuana decreased drastically. He still smokes occasionally when someone offers him a joint at a party, but outside of that, he finds he doesn's need anything to help him get along with his family.

Arthur gets the credit here. He is the one who turned things around. He was able to do that because he wasn't afraid to show both his son and his wife that they were very important to him.

GUILT

Most parents are experts at making their teens feel guilty and using that guilt to manipulate their teens to do things. One of the reasons that some parents are so good at this is that they learned this skill from experts—their parents! These parents find that producing guilt is a way of life and they are not even aware of it most of the time. For example, a mother has spent an afternoon cleaning her 16-year-old son's room and she says to him, "See, look at all I have done for you today!" Her implied message is: "What have you done for me?" Messages like this one make teens feel guilty.

At other times when this same mother is angry, she will throw up to her son what she did for him. For example, "You don't appreciate anything. I spent three hours yesterday (or last week or last month!) cleaning up your room and you just don't care." Her implied message here is: "You ingrate, you—what did I do to deserve such a child?"

Using guilt as a means of getting your teen to do something for you is destructive. First of all, guilt is a tremendously difficult feeling to carry around inside you. Secondly, even if the teen does something for you because he feels guilty, he'll resent it and that resentment coupled with his feelings of guilt can produce terrible feelings of anger.

Sometimes that anger is right on the surface and he can get rid of it—either destructively or constructively; other times, that anger is hidden, buried deep, and therefore more difficult for the teen to identify and express. (See Chapter 11 on Anger)

There are two important rules to remember in

dealing with your teen if you are interested in avoiding feelings of guilt:

1. Do things for your kids because you want to do them. If doing something for your youngster, such as cleaning his room, takes time that you don't want to give, you are better off not doing it. Do things for the joy it brings, not because you think you should.
2. When you're angry at your child, instead of making him feel guilty, send him a STRAIGHT TALK message. It will help you take care of your anger, without giving your child a bag of guilt to carry around.

VALUES

Teenagers don't behave or speak as though they believe in their parents' values. And most times they act and speak this way in an attempt to define for themselves what they do value. As parents we know this, yet when our values and the values of our teens collide, the collision is much more hurtful than we ever realized it would be. Teens need to rebel—to differentiate themselves from us. They need to try on values that are different from their parents' values. They need to become their own person. They need to feel more autonomy. What we as parents have got to do is to find ways that we can live through this period, which, though difficult, is perfectly normal, age-appropriate behavior for the adolescent years.

If we can learn to bend without breaking, if we can learn to be strong when we need to be strong, if we can learn to give when we need to give, then both parents and teens will get through the difficult period of the adolescent years.

When your teen seems to be espousing a value that is different from your own and you can see a values collision in the making we offer you the following guidelines:

1. *Don't Panic.*
   Keep in mind that what your teen is doing is age-appropriate behavior. Panic only serves to polarize those involved in the conflict.
2. *Be a Model.*
   Model the behavior you want your teen to adopt. Modeling is the most potent tool a parent has. Remember, your actions speak louder than your words.
3. *Share Information.*
   Sometimes just exchanging information helps all parties concerned to resolve a values issue. Make sure the information you have is accurate. Some of the information and facts we have given our teens in the past has been inaccurate and parents may find that any new information they have is viewed with suspicion by their teen. Remember, you have your skills—send a STRAIGHT TALK message. Use your ATTENTIVE LISTENING skill. Be non-judgmental and don't use put-downs. Keep in mind that this family wants to be able to live, love and work together as a unit.
4. *Negotiation/Contract.*
   In a negotiation meeting, use your PROBLEM-SOLVING skills. Keep in mind, however, that the solutions generated at such a meeting will mean that everyone involved will lose a little. Certainly, it's far better to lose a little and keep the relationship with your teen than it is to "win" the battle and lose the war, or in this case your relationship with your teen. If negotiation is not your style, try the contract meeting. As long as you and your teen are talking and relating to each other, problems—and values issues—can be resolved.
5. *Houseclean Your Own Values.*
   Maybe it's time to clean out your values closet!

Many of us are carrying around values that we haven't used in years—values that we may have inherited from our own parents that we are passing on to our children. So, check out your own values.

Keep in mind that a values conflict is not the end of the world—although at the time it's happening it may seem to be. More often than not, children espouse the values of their parents by the time they reach adulthood. Values are learned—we are not born with them.

RESPECT

The tone of a household is set by the parents residing within that household. The first step in setting the tone or atmosphere of the household is respect. Respect can only be given, it cannot be commanded of another person.

If you want your teen to show you respect, you must show him respect. Sometimes it's almost impossible to show respect to your teen when there is hardly anything your teen is doing of which you approve. Find something—anything—your teen is doing that you like, and work from there. Maybe your son almost always sinks the ball in the basket when he makes free throws. Maybe your son takes good care of his pets. Maybe your son sticks to a job until it's finished—even if that job is fixing a motorcycle. Whatever the situation, send him a STRAIGHT TALK message that conveys your good feelings. Do the same thing with your spouse—with everyone else in your family. Change the tone of your household to one of affection and appreciation—when you do, respect will follow.

CHAPTER 14

When to Go to the Therapist

Although the general public's attitude toward mental health has been improving greatly in this country in the last twenty years, still, in the eyes of some people, a stigma is associated with seeing a therapist. This, of course, is nonsense.

We feel that everybody in general, and anybody who has an adolescent in particular, should see a therapist any time there is a serious problem, such as depression, poor performance in school, or poor social skills, to name a few. If a member of your family has a medical problem such as a sprained ankle, the measles, or an infection, you don't hesitate to go to a doctor or other expert in the medical field. If someone in your family has a toothache, a cavity, or something wrong with a tooth, you don't hesitate to go to a dentist. We believe that every teenager should see a therapist at least once for a checkup. Going to see a therapist is no different than going to the doctor or the dentist.

The therapist is trained to help people. He or she helps people change the unhappy parts of their lives, and make them happier. He or she helps people with problems to understand and correct those problems.

Don't hesitate to go to a therapist whenever you feel there is a problem in your family that you cannot deal with or that is causing someone serious unhappiness. Even if you think your problem or concern is silly, stupid or dumb, don't hesitate to see a therapist. We would much rather see you go to a therapist and be told that you don't need to be there, than to let a

problem become more severe because then it is usually
more difficult to deal with in therapy. Ninety percent
of the adolescents we see in therapy should have been
brought in sooner than they were. Many parents make
the mistake of thinking, "It's just a phase and he'll
grow out of it," "He's having a bad time now, but
things will get better," or "We'll just wait a little while
longer before we do something."

> *Many parents seem to think that if they ignore
> the problem it will go away. However, it seldom
> does. The problem usually becomes magnified.
> The longer you wait to bring an adolescent with
> a problem to a therapist, the longer it takes to
> correct the problem.*

We can give you some guidelines to use to help
you determine when to bring your teen to a therapist,
but remember, these are just guidelines. When you
suspect there may be a problem, don't hesitate—
make an appointment to see a therapist.

GUIDELINES

1. *School*
   When a teen is doing poorly in school, particularly
   if his grades in elementary school and junior high
   were much better, and then suddenly fall off in
   high school, he should be seen by a therapist.
   When a teen is being disciplined in school for poor
   social behavior, or when he is cutting classes or not
   going to school, he should be seen by a therapist.

2. *Law*
   When a teen does anything that gets him involved
   with the criminal justice system, he should be seen
   by a therapist. If a teen is breaking the law, but
   hasn't been caught yet, he should be seen by a

therapist. Don't assume that boys will be boys and ignore this sign of a problem. When a teen continually gets tickets with his car or has accidents, when he shoplifts, burglarizes homes, does vandalism, steals money from his parents, or the like, he need to see a therapist.

3. *Peers*
When a teen has friends you don't approve of, destructive youngsters who are influencing your teenager with their destructive ways, he needs to see a therapist. If all his friends are like this, chances are he's in with a bad crowd—there is a specific reason for this and a therapist can help find out why.

4. *Drugs*
Any teen who uses amphetamines, barbiturates, PCP (angel dust), cocaine, LSD (acid), heroin, should be RUSHED to a therapist! If you suspect that your youngster is using marijuana check out his behavior: is he showing a lack of responsibility, is he dropping off in school, has he changed his circle of friends? Watch for repeated usages and psychological dependency.

5. *Alcohol*
Watch for the misuse of alcohol, frequent use of alcohol, a lack of control of the amount of alcohol consumed, irrational and irresponsible behavior when using alcohol.

6. *Depression*
Any adolescent who mopes around, feels "down" all the time, doesn't seem to have much energy, says all he's doing is feeling blue, doesn't seem to enjoy life, appears miserable all the time, and just doesn't seem at all happy, should be seen by a therapist. The teen who is lonely and withdrawn, who has difficulty making friends, who seldom goes out on weekends with any friends, who seldom

or never goes to friends' homes, also needs to be seen by a therapist.

7. *Suicidal Thoughts*

IMMEDIATELY see a therapist if your teen talks about ending his life, doing away with himself, says he would be better off dead, that life is not worth living, that he's feeling blue, that he is totally hopeless and his life will never change so he wants to go to sleep and never wake up, says he'll get even with you by killing himself, or any similar statements. A parent doesn't have the training to evaluate a suicidal statement. Go to a professional and let him evaluate such statements. Adolescent suicides are at their highest level ever and the figure climbs higher every year.

8. *Poor Self-Image*

Although it is normal for teens to have doubts about their self-image during adolescence, an extremely poor self-image will affect how a person achieves in school, how a person feels about himself, and how he does later on in life. Any teen who seems not to like himself, who seems down on himself all the time, rarely seems to enjoy himself, whose self-esteem and self-concept seem to be at a dangerously low ebb, should be seen by a therapist.

9. *Hearing Voices or Seeing Things*

This is a very critical item. If your teenager should ever tell you that he thinks people are following him, that he hears voices of other people talking to him, he should be seen by a therapist IMMEDIATELY!

10. *Severe Weight Loss*

If a teen stops eating, loses weight, refuses to eat much of anything, continually tells you that he's

too fat, when in reality he's not at all fat, and
persists in such behavior, he should be taken to
a therapist IMMEDIATELY!

11. *Rebelliousness at Home*
   If a teen is acting more rebellious than normally,
   stomping out of the house when he's angry, staying away for hours at a time, refusing to do any
   chores at all, not cooperating minimally with his
   family, being totally defiant all the time, check
   him out with a therapist.

12. *Sexually Acting Out*
   There are well over one million teenage preg-
   nancies each year. If your teen is having sex, it is
   a good idea to take him to a therapist for a
   general mental health checkup. It is amazing in
   this day and age that so many teens don't know
   the first thing about birth control. What is even
   more amazing is that teens who do know about
   birth control methods, don't use them. These
   teens get pregnant becaues they want to—either
   consciously or unconsciously. They have tremendously low self-esteem. For the teenage girl, getting pregnant in her eyes affirms her femininity,
   makes her feel really like a woman and com-
   pensates for her very low self-esteem. In addition,
   many girls consciously or unconsciously want to
   get pregnant because they want the status of being
   a mother and immaturely feel they are capable of
   it. For the teenage boy, impregnating a girl means
   to him that he's a man, and affirms his masculinity
   since he can get his girl pregnant and this com-
   pensates for his feelings of low self-esteem.

13. *Problems Between Spouses*
   Very often one parent has taken a position that
   the other parent feels is totally unreasonable and

that parent won't budge. Part of the function of therapy is to help educate parents in terms of what is age-appropriate behavior for teens and what is appropriate behavior for parents.

14. *Parent-in-the-Middle*
We discussed in Chapter 13 the tremendous problem faced by the parent who finds himself in the middle of the conflict between the other parent and the adolescent. A therapist can offer help and insight into these situations.

15. *Loners*
Teens who are withdrawn, have few or no friends, who spend large amounts of time alone, should be seen by a therapist.

16. *Problems Between Family Members*
If youngsters refuse to problem-solve or enter into a contract meeting, or families are not able to resolve problems using these methods, they should see a therapist.

These are some of the major reasons and criteria parents should use in deciding when to go to the therapist. However, they are by no means all-inclusive and you should remember that the time to go to the therapist is when you suspect there is a problem that isn't being handled well by one or more members of your family. You need to remember, too, that what you're doing is simply consulting an expert about a problem.
It is important also to be aware of why people are resistant to going to therapy. The following section examines some of the major types of resistance to therapy and makes some suggestions on how you can overcome these types of resistance.

RESISTANCE *

1. *Resistance Due To Feeling Guilty.*

One of the major forms of resistance on the part of parents is their feelings of guilt. When they acknowledge that their teen has a problem of any type that requires therapy, they frequently believe that they are automatically "bad" parents. The dynamics behind this thought is: "If I had been a good parent my teen would not need to go to a therapist."

When this happens, parents frequently deny a problem exists. Remind yourself that if your child had a medical problem you wouldn't hesitate to go to a doctor, or if he had a dental problem you wouldn't hesitate to go to the dentist, so why not seek the help of an expert—a therapist—in the mental health field.

Another way to deal with this problem of feeling guilty is to remember that even if parents were perfect, teens would still have problems because part of what happens to them as they grow up is determined by how they interpret their parents' actions, and by how a teen interprets and meets the environment as well as peer group pressure.

2. *Resistance Due To A Feeling Of Being Punished.*

Sometimes parents see therapy as a punishment. They believe that because their teen has a problem, they are going to have to spend money for therapy and they may be asked to go with their teen, so therefore, they think they are being punished in terms of time and money—and for something that isn't their fault!

One way to deal with this resistance is to ac-

---

* Buntman, Peter H., M.S.W., ACSW, and Wenner, David, M.S.W., *Dealing With Assistance to Therapy*, unpublished, 1977.

knowledge how angry you are and to recognize that this anger is directed at your teen. Once you acknowledge the anger and the fact that it is unfair, that it isn't right, that it is unjust, then you can say, "Yes, all of these things are true, but there is a problem. Let's try to solve it by going to therapy."

3. *Resistance Due To Attitudes About Mental Health.*
Many parents resist going to therapy because of antiquated ideas they have that only "sicko," "psycho," or "nutty" people go to therapists. They can sometimes give examples of someone in their family who went to therapy—"Aunt Sally went through therapy and she was a psycho all her life!" Some parents also believe that if a person is really strong enough, he can solve his own problems.

If you have this type of resistance it is important to know that, for the most part, there is no great difference between people who go to therapists and people who don't. The people who do are taking responsibility for their own lives, and they are seeking to live happier, fuller, more satisfying lives.

4. *Resistance Due To Embarrassment.*
A surprisingly large number of people who can accept the fact that they need therapy are embarrassed about letting other poeple know—even family members—that they are in therapy. Some people are often worried that someone in the community may see them going in and out of a therapist's office. They also worry that neighbors, employers, friends, and relatives will somehow find out they are seeing a therapist.

To deal with this form of resistance, it is important to know that anything you discuss with your therapist—even your name—is strictly confidential. It is totally your business—if you don't want to tell anyone that you're going to a therapist, don't.

5. *Resistance Due To The Feeling Of Having A Threatening Experience.*

People usually feel comfortable even though often troubled, in their patterns of behavior and the way they relate to each other. They know that in therapy they will be asked to look at those patterns of behavior, the way they relate to other people. Because of this they think that making changes may be scary, threatening and uncomfortable. Sometimes people are worried that some deep, dark secret will be uncovered.

In dealing with this form of resistance, it is important to understand what actually happens during therapy. Most of the time, a person sees his therapist once a week. Each session or meeting lasts from 45 to 50 minutes. A person talks about the problem areas in his life and talks about those parts of his life that are unhappy. A therapist helps that person understand his behavior—why he is exhibiting that behavior.

When you go to a doctor with an infection, he may give you some pills. If you follow the doctor's directions and take your medication, you generally get better. In therapy, a therapist can't *make* you better and can't always tell you what to do, but he *can* help you understand and help yourself. If you are willing to participate by talking about your life and your problems, and are willing to look at your behavior, a therapist can help you help yourself.

Uncomfortable at times? Yes, possibly. But it can also be very exciting to understand more about you and in that process learn new ways of relating to people and to yourself that should result in making you and the members of your family happier.

6. *Resistance Due To Delay.*

Many times people will say they need therapy, agree to go see a therapist and then will not do

anything more than that. Another delaying tactic
is to postpone the undertaking, using such excuses
as, "I'll call a therapist right after the holidays,"
or "I'll start therapy in a month or so when I finish
my class at college," or "When we get back from
our summer vacation, we're going to get right into
therapy," or "As soon as my husband finishes a
big project he has at work." And, of course, they
never get started.

Usually resistance due to delay is coupled with
one or more of the other reasons we've already
mentioned. If you find you're putting off starting
therapy, we suggest you look carefully at all the
reasons for resisting therapy.

7. *Resistance Due To A Lack Of Money.*
Many people will resist going to therapy because
they think they can't afford it and that it's too
expensive. Certainly therapy isn't cheap. But when
you consider the years of training, postgraduate
work, and the educational level of therapists,
you're paying for highly trained and qualified
professionals.

Sometimes parents feel embarrassed about their
financial situation and therefore put off starting
therapy. We want to encourage families to approach
the therapist of their choice, check out his cost. If
you can't afford his cost, ask the therapist to recommend someone who is in private practice or an
agency whose cost you can afford. It may be that
group therapy would be the therapy of choice, and
group therapy is less expensive than individual
therapy. Almost all communities have free clinics,
county facilities or agencies which charge accord-
ing to a person's ability to pay. These agencies are
supported by tax dollars and are there for people
to use.

Many times parents recognize the need for
therapy, but their adolescent refuses to attend. In

fact, the adolescent denies that he has a problem. Denying that he has problems is one way adolescents deal with their inadequacies. It is important to remember, though, the adolescent REALLY BELIEVES his denial.

If this is the situation, we suggest that you talk to your adolescent about therapy in terms of the analogy we used earlier in this chapter. You go to a doctor when there is a medical problem, a dentist when there is a dental problem, and a counselor-therapist when there is a problem within the family and the family is unhappy. If the adolescent is still resisting, as often happens, and adamantly refuses to go, we suggest you try to negotiate the following agreement with him by saying something like, "Look, we're really concerned, we see a problem in the family. We all want to go to the therapist and we want you to come with us." Suggest that your teen attend once a week for six weeks. "It is only an hour a week and it will be for only six weeks—all you have to lose is six hours out of your life. What you have to gain is that it might make some of the unhappy parts of your life happier. If at the end of six weeks you don't want to continue, you don't have to."

If at the end of six weeks some type of relationship is not established between the adolescent and the therapist, the therapy usually won't be very successful. So, in attempting this, there is minimal risk for the parents.

How Do You Choose A Therapist?

There are many different types of therapists in terms of their educational training, different belief systems or models of psychotherapy, and personalities of individuals. The interaction between the therapist and the client is more important in this professional relationship than almost any other. In choosing a family therapist we suggest you use the following criteria, and in addition, that these criteria be discussed with the therapist:

1. You should get "good vibes" from the therapist—that means that he seems to care about YOU and that you are not just #6 or #8 on the list that day. He should be concerned and interested in you as well as interested in his work. If you don't find these "good vibes" with one therapist, we suggest that you look for another.

2. You should ask him if he has a license to practice therapy. Some highly qualified but non-licensed therapists work directly under a licensed therapist. Find out what your state requirements are and make sure the therapist you choose meets those requirements.

3. You should ask him about his educational background.

4. You should ask him what experience he has had working with teenagers, and whether or not he has had any graduate or post-graduate training preparing him for this specialized work.

5. You should ask him what percentage of his practice is spent with teenagers and their families. Remember you are looking for someone who has had lots of experience working with teenagers and who sees teenagers in his practice all the time. In other words, you are looking for someone who specializes in working with adolescents and their families.

The Different Types of Therapists

There are four major types of therapists: clinical or psychiatric social workers, psychologists, marriage, family and child counselors, and psychiatrists.

These different types of therapists have graduate schools throughout the nation, they have national associations which set standards of practice for each respective discipline, and they have national criteria for the level and quality of the graduate training.

While there are many other people who do therapy, only the four types of therapists above have national accrediting bodies for graduate schools as well as graduate schools around the country. You are assured of a high quality of education and training since the graduate schools of each of these professions are accredited and have high national standards.

CLINICAL OR PSYCHIATRIC SOCIAL WORKERS

The term "social worker" has been a confusing one for the public. This term can be applied to the social worker who works in the welfare department, as well as the social worker who practices therapy. To clarify the confusion, all social workers who are licensed to practice therapy in their respective states must have a graduate professional degree called an "M.S.W. degree." When a candidate receives that degree, it means he has successfully completed a graduate professional training program in a graduate school of social work. Social workers who have this degree usually call themselves psychiatric or clinical social workers. Most social workers who practice therapy also belong to the Academy of Certified Social Workers and use the letters ACSW. This certifies that after 2,000 hours of supervised experience following graduate school they have passed a national test to earn the designation of ACSW. Clinical or psychiatric social workers statistically do more therapy than any other profession. They work in many diverse fields, so be sure to choose one who has specialized training in the field of family and adolescent counseling.

PSYCHOLOGISTS

Psychologists are trained in graduate schools of psychology and have either a Masters Degree (M.A.

or M.S.) or a doctorate (Ph.D.). Usually qualifications for psychologists who are licensed for private practice include two years of supervised experience plus licensing requirements in the state in which they are licensed to practice therapy. Psychologists work in many fields, so in choosing one to be a therapist for your family make sure his interest and study is in the field of family and adolescent counseling. Psychologists also have specialized training in educational and psychological testing.

Marriage, Family and Child Counselors

Marriage, Family, and Child Counselors are licensed in the following six states: California, Georgia, Michigan, Nevada, New Jersey and Utah. Marriage, Family and Child Counselors have specialized skills in understanding how people relate to each other, in communication and communication problems, and in the family and the family system. Although Marriage, Family and Child Counselors have excellent backgrounds in working with families, be sure to choose one who has an interest and background in working with adolescents.

Psychiatrists

Psychiatrists are always medical doctors who have had additional training as psychotherapists. They have an M.D. degree and in addition have many hours of additional study and supervised experience, much of which is in psychiatric hospitals. Psychiatrists also work in many fields, so in choosing one to be a therapist for your family make sure his interest and background is in the field of family and adolescent counseling. Psychiatrists are the only therapists who can prescribe medicine.

WHERE DO YOU LOOK FOR A THERAPIST?

Once you have made the decision to see a therapist, the next step is to find one. We recommend the best way to choose a therapist is to ask your junior high or your high school counselor. He knows the names of professionals to whom he has referred students and their families, who are specialists in adolescent and family therapy. If for any reason your school counselor doesn't have names to give you, call the district office and ask for the district psychologist or social worker and ask him for referrals. Another good source of referrals is your family doctor. He also may know adolescent and family therapists. Your church or temple, or your local mental health agency also can supply you with a referral list. Some cities also have organizations which provide information, evaluation and referral services.

Check your telephone directory for the local telephone numbers of the state professional associations for clinical or psychiatric social workers, psychologists, or psychiatrists—they will also furnish you with a referral list.

The next step is up to you. Make some phone calls, set up some appointments and then carefully choose your therapist.

CHAPTER 15

Questions from Parents

What did I do wrong? I must have goofed up very badly because my kid has problems.

After reading this book you may wish that you had done certain things differently. Also, you may wish you hadn't done some things at all, However, if you use the skills that are outlined in this book, you have the opportunity now to make some changes in the way you relate to your teen. It is often difficult for a therapist to determine what a parent did "wrong" specifically—therapists are much better at "fixing up a problem" than in determining exactly and specifically "what went wrong."

What we can tell you is that even if you were "perfect" parents, your adolescent would still experience problems. By the way, we don't think there is such a thing as a "perfect" parent. We're all human and therefore subject to the human phenomenon of making a mistake now and then!

So, the problems encountered by adolescents are not there because of "imperfect" parents, but rather because of a youngster's reaction to his environment —how he perceives it, experiences it, and internalizes it—and his reaction to his parents. All of these factors enter into the "problem." We feel that it is important, too, that you as a parent make a decision. Are you going to keep torturing yourself about what went wrong in the past, or are you going to make some changes? The skills outlined in this book will help you make those changes.

Why does one of my children have a lot of problems and the others seem okay? This is so hard to understand because we treated them all the same.

Despite the fact that you treated all of your children the same, each child has a separate and unique experience growing up in a family by virtue of his numerical position in the family. A first child for part of his life is an only child until a second child arrives. A second child grows up with someone older than he is for his whole life. A third child grows up with two children who are older than he is. So, you can see that where a child is placed in a family, makes for different experiences which create a different living situation. Each child reacts differently, so some experience "problems" and some do not.

Should teens have chores?

Definitely, yes. It helps give them a sense of responsibility and helps prepare them for the world outside the family. The sense of accomplishment that comes from doing a job well is a great self-esteem builder.

Is it my fault that my teenager has a problem?

No, not necessarily. Read our answer to the first question and remember that there is no such thing as a "perfect" parent—and even if there were, some youngsters would still have problems. Each youngster deals with his life in his own special way and he interprets what his parents do in his own special way. For example, a child may experience strong love from both parents, and believe that the only way he can keep their love is to accomplish certain things. Because he interprets their love in that way may cause him problems at some point in his life.

I can't control my 14-year-old son. Am I responsible for what he does?

While you may not be able to *control* him, you

certainly can *influence* him. We suggest you read this book carefully and use the skills outlined. Your responsibility for your son, in a legal sense, ends when he becomes of age. Each state defines legal responsibility for children in different ways. This information can be obtained from your local state agencies.

I think my son's smoking pot. How can I tell for sure? What can I do about it?

If you have a good relationship with your son, ask him. If you don't, you can try to build up better rapport between you. You can do this by using the communication skills in this book. We believe that misuse or abuse of any drug or chemical is a symptom of an underlying problem. If you can sit down and discuss the subject with him, you can perhaps find out what the underlying problem is.

My daughter thinks I'm the dumbest person in the whole world. How can I make her understand that I don't want her to make the same mistakes that I did?

You have set yourself an impossible task. You may have to accept the fact that you are helpless in some areas. This will probably make you feel both angry and sad. One of the greatest tests of a parent's skill in caring is that he can love his adolescent enough to let him make his own mistakes. Other than sending Straight Talk messages, modeling the behavior you want your daughter to follow and listening to her, there is not much more you can do. You have to love your teen enough to allow her to make her own mistakes. Make your home a place of refuge and nurturing love and your teen will make her way home over and over again with an instinct of a homing pigeon!

Why won't my teenager do things with the family?

Not wanting to do things with the family and needing to spend some time away from the family is normal for an adolescent. Include your teen by inviting him to go along with the family but don't expect his company each time. If there are times you insist upon his going with the family, talk over with him the reasons why, and allow him the freedom to choose whether or not to go with you other times instead.

How can I make my daughter go to church?

Other than using extreme force, you may not be able to. We believe that teens should have some choice in deciding their values and you may have to accept the fact that your teen has a different value about church than you do. Remember, she's a teen, not a child, and her beliefs are valid to her at this time. In the future, her beliefs *may* match yours more closely, if she has the freedom of choice now.

In the meantime, avoid calling her names or putting her down because her values differ from yours. Frequently, teens "try on" values that are very different from their parents and then quickly return to their old values.

My daughter is stealing money from me and telling me lies. Nothing I've done is helping. What can I do?

Stealing money and telling lies are ways a teenager unconsciously uses to ask for help. They are distress flags—and parents need to be alert for signs such as these. We strongly urge you to read the chapter on "How to Choose a Therapist," and find one with whom you can discuss your concerns.

My daughter wants to go on the pill. She's only 15 years old. I don't want her to become sexually active yet. How can I make her understand that she's got her whole life ahead of her?

Talk to her. Tell her why you feel the way you do. Listen to what she has to say in reply. If she still wants to go on the pill, consider her request. See to it that she has the birth control information she needs. Tell her what your values are and while you wish they were hers also, she has a right to her own values. The important thing to remember here is to keep open the lines of communication between you and your daughter.

I think maybe my son is a homosexual. How can I tell for sure? What can I do to help him?

The whole area of adolescent sexuality can be very confusing. There is a big difference between homosexuality and statistically normal adolescent homosexual experiences. Research shows that over 75% of adolescent boys have at least one homosexual experience in adolescence. If you have any serious concerns, see a therapist and discuss those concerns with him/her.

My daughter is making up lies about her stepfather. I know they are not true. He wouldn't do things like that. How can I put a stop to these lies?

First of all, we suggest that you really listen to your daughter and hear what she's saying. You need to be ABSOLUTELY sure that what she's telling you are lies. Check out what she says before you make that decision. If you are 100% satisfied that they are lies, then try to listen to the feelings behind those lies. Use your Listening skill and let your daughter express those feelings and talk them out with you. Typical feelings that she will be trying to express will be anger, resentment and jealousy.

If you find that your daughter is telling the truth, then you must make some difficult decisions immediately. Your daughter needs your protection as well as counseling and your husband should seek the help of a qualified therapist without delay.

My 17-year-old son is definitely hooked on drugs. Will it do any good to send him to live with my sister in Phoenix?

Probably not. His drug usage is symptomatic of

some underlying problems and simply changing environments without dealing with and treating the underlying problems seldom produces change. In our clinical experience, when parents change the environment without providing treatment, they are amazed that within a couple of days, their teen is able to find drug-using friends at a new school in a new city. Again, we suggest that the crucial thing is to deal with the problem directly and with the help of a qualified therapist.

I have been concerned about the fact that my neighbor's son has joined a weird cult. What can my neighbor do for her son and what can I do to prevent this same thing happening to my daughter?

If your neighbor's son has joined a cult or group and is over 18 years of age, there isn't much that can be done. We are assuming, of course, that he freely associated himself with this group or cult. Usually people join cults or groups because it gives them an easy out. All they have to do is believe in the "message" of the cult and they don't have to face the world and all its problems. And, of course, they don't have to deal with people. They don't even have to think. So, for a confused, troubled, insecure adolescent, you can see its attraction. It offers security, serenity, and promises to take care of the person. What is really difficult for each of us, including teenagers and adults, is to face reality each day and deal with the problems of work, friends, and family.

The best way you can insure that your daughter won't join a cult is to provide her with a secure family and a happy home where the doors of communication are always open.

My daughter has been feeling very down and blue lately. She has said things like "life isn't worth living," "I'm thinking about ending it all," and "I'd be better off dead." What should I do?

While it is age-appropriate behavior for adolescents to feel down and depressed at times, any talk of suicide, or statements such as your daughter has made should be evaluated by a therapist IMMEDIATELY. Parents do not have the knowledge to assess the validity of suicidal statements and they should, as soon as they hear them, immediately make an appointment with a therapist.

My daughter is overweight. Nothing we do will get her to lose weight. We have promised her a vacation in Hawaii if she loses weight and lots of other things. She is obviously unhappy because she's so fat that I could cry!

We put obesity into the category of substance abuse. She is abusing food just as other teenagers abuse drugs or alcohol. The abuse of food and the consequent obesity are symptomatic of an underlying problem. You will probably need to take her to a therapist and get professional help to help her deal with that problem. Once the underlying problem is dealt with in therapy, then the symptom can be alleviated.

How do I know when my son is an adolescent? What things should I look for emotionally? My son is 12 years old.

You can assume that any 12-year-old is already into adolescence. We define the years of adolescence as being 12 through 20. Because of the pressures of our society, we see 11½-year-olds and 11-year-olds displaying adolescent behavior. Reread Chapter 2 which tells you what to expect emotionally of an adolescent.

How can I tell if I should be overly concerned about my son's behavior? I don't know what's normal and what's not.

The answer to this question can also be found in Chapter 2. It will give you some guidelines which you can apply to your adolescent.

I had a terrible time during my teen years. I don't want my children to have a bad time. What can I do to make sure they don't?

You can use the skills, methods and ideas that we suggest in this book. Parents who can communicate with their adolescent and who can love and understand them are better able to help their teen through adolescence with as much strength and as little discomfort as possible.

My daughter has befriended a girl I don't approve of. I'm sure she's a bad type. What can I do to break up this friendship before it's too late?

This is a tough one. You will probably be most successful if you express your feelings in strong Straight Talk messages early in the relationship. You may even want to, at that time, forbid the relationship. Keep in mind, however, that because of a teen's need to rebel and because of peer group influence, forbidding such a relationship may be a difficult task. This kind of friend is important to your daughter right now and if you are successful in stopping this friendship, another one may soon appear. It might be helpful to try to find out why your daughter needs this type of friend—what the attraction is—and then help her deal with that need.

My daughter came home from a party smelling of liquor. We don't drink and don't want her to drink. She's always been such a good girl and I'm afraid she's going to get mixed up with the wrong crowd. What can I do to prevent that from happening?

It sounds like this was an experimental type of behavior and you can use your communication skills to express your feelings and to listen to your daughter's feelings. Remember, the misuse of alcohol is symptomatic of an underlying problem. It is a good time to take stock of the situation and see if indeed there is a problem here or only experimentation is involved.

My oldest son was killed in an auto accident six months ago. His youngest sister is lost without him. She's lost her appetite, she's listless, she doesn't sleep well, and she doesn't have any interest in school and her friends. I can't seem to reach her. What can I do?

She's depressed and is grieving about the death of her brother. Her depression is at a point where she really needs the help of a therapist. Reread Chapter 14 for some guidelines on how to choose a therapist.

We have four children; three of them get along pretty well, but one (second child) seems to push the others the wrong way. I have tried everything. What do you suggest?

Try the problem-solving approaches—both the family meeting and the contract meeting (Chapters 8 and 9, respectively). If that doesn't work, it's time to seek a therapist.

Is it true that siblings have to fight?

Because children and teens need attention from their parents and because they are jealous of each other, they will fight. It is normal for them to do some fighting. As a parent you need to recognize this but also continue to teach them how to live with and get along with each other.

CHAPTER 16

Institutes for Adolescent Studies

One of the goals of our book is for parents to learn new skills in relating to their children and to each other. For a few parents reading this book may provide all the help that is necessary. For others a more intensive and personal educational experience may be needed or desired. To meet that goal, we are establishing Institutes for Adolescent Studies throughout the country. It is our hope that parents will come to these Institutes to attend classes in order to learn interpersonal skills that will not only enrich their lives, but the lives of each family member.

Each local Institute for Adolescent Studies offers a class entitled "How To Live With Your Teenager." This class, which teaches parenting skills, meets one night a week for six weeks. Each meeting is two hours. The class is completed in twelve hours.

The class, "How To Live With Your Teenager," will teach such topics as age-appropriate behaviors, why communication stops and how to start it again, listening skills, body language, how to raise self-esteem, self-esteem quizzes, straight talk skills, how to praise, how to criticize, the importance of time and touch, problem-solving skills, the contract meeting, anger, additional tips for parents, and more.

The format of the class will include lectures, discussions, and practice of the skills. One of the key learning tools for the class will be a specially designed workbook which will be given to every class member. Each person will have the opportunity during the six-week program to practice the new skills he or she is learning.

Each person who attends the six-week program will be meeting other parents of teenagers who have the same or similar concerns.

We would be happy to have you share with us any comments you may have about the book. We look forward to sharing our future books with you.

A life that is fulfilling and happy is available to each of us. We have only to care enough to seek it. The seeking of it requires the effort, the time, and the willingness to try something new.

The following are the names, addresses, and telephone numbers of the Institutes for Adolescent Studies. If there is not one close to you, please write us at:

INSTITUTE FOR ADOLESCENT STUDIES
311 So. San Gabriel Blvd.
Pasadena, California 91107
(213) 795-0208

We will refer you to the Institute that is closest to you since new ones will be opening soon throughout the United States.

If you wish to be on our mailing list to receive special announcements for parents of teenagers, please mail the attached card. If the card is not in your copy of the book, write your name, address, and telephone on a piece of paper with the word "Announcements" on it, and mail it to our address.

CALIFORNIA

Peter H. Buntman, M.S.W., ACSW, Clinical Director
Eleanor M. Saris, M.Ed., Executive Director
3422 Yellowtail Drive
Los Alamitos, California 90720   (213) 596-8712

Peter H. Buntman, M.S.W., ACSW, Clinical Director
Eleanor M. Saris, M.Ed., Executive Director
3120 So. Hacienda Heights Blvd., #202 A&B
Hacienda Heights, California 91745   (213) 330-0089

Peter H. Buntman, M.S.W., ACSW, Clinical Director
Eleanor M. Saris, M.Ed., Executive Director
2700 Bellflower Boulevard, Suite 315
Long Beach, California 90815   (213) 596-8712

Peter H. Buntman, M.S.W., ACSW, Clinical Director
Eleanor M. Saris, M.Ed., Executive Director
315 So. San Gabriel Boulevard
Pasadena, California 91107   (213) 795-0208

David McCann, Ph.D., M.F.C.C., Director
Janis McCann, M.F.C.C., Director
761 Latimer Road
Santa Monica, California 90402   (213) 459-3139

CONNECTICUT

Robert F. Nottage, M.S.W., ACSW, Director
657 Wiese Road
Cheshire, Connecticut 06410   (203) 272-9774

Richard Krafcik, M.A., M.F.C.C., Director
361 Reeds Gap Road
Northford, Connecticut 06472

MASSACHUSETTS

Brockton Area Multi-Services, Inc.
Attn: Carol Stokes
165 Quincy Street
Brockton, Massachusetts 02402   (617) 588-7388

Paul Tausek, M.S.W., ACSW, Executive Director
Frederick J. Welsh, M.Ed., Clinical Director
Beverly A. Elliott, M.Ed., Clinical Director
4 Taunton Street (Route 152)
Plainville, Massachusetts 02762   (617) 695-0543

MISSOURI

Yitzchok Abramson, Ph.D., Director
Woodsmill 40 Medical Center
14377 Woodlake Drive, #212
Chesterfield, Missouri 63017   (314) 576-7455

NEW YORK

Edward S. Stark, Ph.D., Director
Lillian Demos, M.S., M.Ed., Co-Director
Elaine Schaefer, M.S.W., Co-Director
Leonard Schaefer, M.B.A., Co-Director
684 Broadway
Massapequa, New York 11758   (516) 795-2477

WISCONSIN

Jeffrey Knepler, M.S.W., ACSW, Director
13160 Burleigh Road
Brookfield, Wisconsin 53005   (414) 783-5222

TRAINERS

CALIFORNIA

Mr. Frank Jackson
246 Beresford
Redwood City, CA 94061
(415) 368-5368

Mr. Stephen Lahmann
932 West Howard
Visalia, CA 93277
(209) 733-3493

COLORADO

Dr. Bernard Brown
Joyce Brown
145 Manhattan Drive

Boulder, CO 80303
(303) 494-2328

FLORIDA

Wesley L. Rouse
Warner South College
Lake Wales, FL 33853
(813) 638-1426

ILLINOIS

Dr. Russell Getz
4450 North Mozart
Chicago, IL 60625
(312) 539-3987

Rev. John Kalayil
303 West Barry Ave.
Chicago, IL 60657
(312) 477-5912

Mr. Jack Cole
365 North Oregon
Morton, IL 61550
(309) 263-8577

MAINE

Richard A. Pare
Bangor Community
   College
Eastport Hall
Bangor, Maine
(207) 945-6391

MARYLAND

Rabbi Isaac Lowenbraun
5815 Narcissus Ave.
Baltimore, MD 21215
(301) 578-0489

Beth Murnane
Baltimore County Police
   Dept.
7209 Belair Rd.
Baltimore, MD 21206
(301) 668-7673

MASSACHUSETTS

Dr. T. Oya Benn
273 Dudley Street
Boston, MA 02119
(617) 445-9160

MICHIGAN

Dr. R. Frederick Wacker
1510 Westminster
Ann Arbor, MI 48104
(313) 761-2770

Winifred R. Wood
30603 Pebblestone Ct.
Birmingham, MI 48010
(313) 646-4423

MISSOURI

Lavanda Booth
401 West Walnut
Independence, MO 64050
(816) 836-8743

NEBRASKA

Rev. John B. Cox
902 South Beadle
Papillion, NE 60846
(402) 339-2389

NEW JERSEY

Rev. Justin E. Dzikowicz
St. Paul's Abbey
Newton, NJ 07860
(201) 729-6125

OHIO

Rhonda J. Richardson
589 East North Broadway
Columbus, OH 43214
(614) 262-1149

VIRGINIA

Jane J. Davis
3806 Hillcrest Lane
Annandale, VA 22003
(703) 280-2324

WASHINGTON

Sister Joyce M. Cox BVM
7220 Ford Drive N.W.
Gig Harbor, WA 98335
(206) 265-3609

CANADA

Mimi Khurana
Children's Aid Society
Brantford, Canada
(519) 756-7059

INDIA

Rev. John Kalayil
SVD. Provincial House
510, 32nd Road
Bombay, 400050 India

Positive Feeling Words

accelerated
acceptable
accepted
accepting
accommodating
accustomed
adamant
adequate
admired
adventurous
affected
affectionate
alive
almighty
amazed
ambivalent
amiable
amused
animated
anxious
appreciated
appreciative
approving
assured
astonished
astounded
at-peace
attached
attentive
attractive

awed

beatific
beautiful
best
better
bewitched
blissful
bold
brave
breathless
bright
broadminded
bubbly
buoyant

calm
capable
captivated
carefree
caring
cared for
challenged
charismatic
charmed
cheerful
childish
childlike
clever
close

comfortable
committed
compassionate
competent
competitive
composed
confident
concerned
conscientious
conservative
considerate
considered
consoled
convinced
contented
contrite
cooperative
cordial
courageous
coy
cozy
creative
curious

daring
dedicated
delirious
delighted
delightful
deserving

desirable
desirous
determined
different
diffuse
diminished
distracted
dumbstruck
dutiful

eager
ecstatic
effective
effervescent
elated
electrified
empathetic
enamoured
enchanted
energetic
enjoy
enjoyment
enlightened
enraptured
enriched
enthralled
enthusiastic
entranced
euphoric
excited
exhilarated
expressive

facile
fair
faithful
famished
fantastic
fascinated
fawning

feminine
fervid
feted
flabbergasted
flexible
flustered
foolish
fortunate
free
friendly
frivolous
fulfilled
full
funny

gay
generous
gentle
giddy
glad
glamorous
good
graceful
gracious
grateful
gratified
great
gregarious
groovy

handsome
happy
harmless
healthy
heavenly
helpful
high
honest
honored
hopeful

humbled
hospitable
humorous

immortal
important
impressed
included
incorruptible
incredible
indebted
independent
infatuated
inflexible
informed
insightful
inspired
integrity
intelligent
interested
intimate
intoxicated
intrigued
invigorated
involved

jolly
joyful
joyous
jubilant
jumpy
justified

keen
kicky
kind

lean
liberal
liked

lively
looked-up-to
lovable
love
loved
lovely
loving
loyal
lucky

magical
masculine
masterful
mature
missed
mixed emotions
modest
motivated
mysterious
mystical
mystified

natural
needed
nice

open
optimistic
outgoing
overjoyed
overpowered
overwhelmed

passionate
patient
peaceful
pensive
perceptive
perfectionistic
perplexed

persuaded
pleasant
pleased
poised
popular
positive
powerful
prepared
pretty
productive
prosperous
protected
protective
proud
purposeful

quiet

rambunctious
rational
reassured
receptive
refreshed
relaxed
religious
relieved
remembered
respectful
responsible
responsive
revered
reverent
revitalized
rewarded
rich
right
righteous
romantic

safe

sanctioned
sated
satisfied
saturated
secure
seductive
self-confident
sensational
sensitive
sensuous
sentimental
serene
serious
settled
sexy
shy
silly
sincere
sleepy
smart
smooth
sociable
solemn
solitary
speechless
spiritual
startled
stimulated
strong
stuffed
successful
super
superior
sure
supported
supportive
surprised
surprising
suspense
sympathetic

tactful
talkative
talented
tantalized
tearful
tender
tenderness
tense
tentative
terrific
thankful
thoughtful
thrilled
toasted
tolerant
touched
tranquil
transcendent
transcending
transparent
transported

triumphant
trusted
trusting
truthworthy
tuned-in
turned-on

unbelievable
understanding
understood
unencumbered
uninhibited
unique
uplifted
useful

vibrant
victorious
virile
vital
vitality

vivacious
vixen
voluptuous

wanted
warm
warmed
willing
wise
wiser
wishful
wonderful
wondering
worthy

zany
zealous
zenith
zestful
zippy

Negative Feeling Words

abandoned
abnormal
abrasive
accused
adamant
afflicted
affronted
afraid
aggravated
aggressive
agitated
agony
alarmed
alienated
alone
angry
annoyed
antagonistic
anxious
apart
apathetic
apologetic
appalled
argumentative
ashamed
assailed
at-a-loss
attacked
awkward

bad

badgered
baffled
banished
battered
beat
beaten
befuddled
belittled
bent
betrayed
bitter
blamed
blind
boorish
bored
bothered
brassy
browbeaten
burdened
burned-up
by-passed

caged
callous
castigated
careless
caught
censored
chained
challenged
cheap

cheated
chicken
childish
chilly
closeminded
clumsy
cold
combative
competitive
condemned
confused
conned
conspicuous
contrary
controlled
cornered
corrupted
cranky
crazy
crestfallen
crippled
critical
crooked
cross
cruel
crushed
culpable
cunning

dawdy
dead

165

deadly
deaf
debilitated
deceitful
defeated
defenseless
defiant
dejected
demented
dependent
depressed
deprived
despair
desperate
despised
destructive
disappointed
disapproved (of)
discontented
discouraged
discriminated
 (against)
disdain
diseased
disgruntled
disgusted
dishonest
disloyal
dismayed
distant
distasteful
distracted
distraught
distrust
disturbed
diverted
divided
dominated
doubtful

down in-the-
 dumps
dreadful
dreary
dubious
dumb

embarrassed
emotional
empty
endemic
enervated
enraged
envious
erratic
evil
exasperated
exhausted

false
fawning
fear
fearful
fed-up
flabbergasted
floundering
flustered
foolish
forgetful
forgotten
frantic
friendless
fright
frightened
frustrated
funky
furious
fury
futility

garrulous
gauche
gimpy
gloomy
greedy
grief
guilty
gullible
gypped

handicapped
hardened
harebrained
harmful
harassed
harried
hate
hateful
hellish
helpless
hemmed in
hesitant
homesick
hopeless
horrible
horrified
hostile
hot
hotheaded
humiliated
hungry
hurt
hypocritical
hysterical

idiotic
ignorant
ignored
imbecilic

immature
impatient
imposed upon
inadequate
incapacitated
incestuous
incompetent
inconsiderate
inconsequential
indignant
ineffective
inferior
infuriated
inhibited
insecure
insensitive
insignificant
insincere
insulted
interrupted
intimidated
intolerant
irrational
irresponsible
irritated
isolated

jaded
jagged
jangled
jarred
jaundiced
jealous
jeopardized
jerky
jiggled
jilted
jittery
jolted
jostled

joyless
judged
juggled
jumpy

kayoed
keyed-up
kicked-around
kneaded
knifed
knocked-out
knotted-up
kooky

lacking
laconic
lazy
lecherous
left-out
let-down
licentious
lonely
longing
lost
low
lukewarm
lunging
lustful

mad
maligned
managed
maneuvered
manipulated
maudlin
mean
meaningless
meddlesome
melancholy
misdirected

miserable
mistaken
misunderstood
mixed-up
morbid
moronic
morose
mortified
mute
myopic

narrow
narrow-minded
nasty
naughty
nearsighted
negative
neglected
nervous
niggardly
numb
nutty

obligated
obnoxious
obsessed
odd
odorous
opposed
out-of-it
out-of-place
outraged
outlawed
overburdened
overloaded
overlooked
overwhelmed
overworked

pain

pained
panicked
panicky
parsimonious
passive
paralyzed
perplexed
persecuted
perverse
perverted
petrified
perturbed
pessimistic
pestered
picked-on
pitiful
pity
placated
pooped
poor
powerless
precarious
prejudiced
pressured
prim
prissy
provincial
provoked
punished
put-down
put-upon
put-up-with
puzzled

quarrelsome
queasy
queer

radical
rage

raspy
rebellious
regretful
rejected
repelled
reprehensible
repugnance
repulsed
remorse
resentful
resentments
resigned
resistant
resistive
restless
restrained
retarded
ridiculed
ridiculous
rotten
ruptive
rushed

sad
scared
scattered
scheming
scorned
screwed-up
seething
self-conscious
servile
shaky
shamed
shattered
shocked
shook
shrewish
shunned
shut-off

shut-out
sick
skeptical
slighted
sloppy
smelly
smothered
sneaky
solemn
sorrowful
sorry
spiteful
square
stiff
stingy
strange
stuck
stumped
stupid
stupefied
stunned
stymied
submissive
subversive
suffering
sunk
suspicious

tearful
teed-off
tempted
tenacious
tenuous
tense
terrible
terrified
terror
thoughtless
threatened
thwarted

timid
tired
tongue-tied
tormented
torn
tortured
toxic
trapped
traumatized
tricked
troubled
turned-off
twisted

ugly
unacceptable
unaccustomed
unappreciated
uncaring
uncertain
uncomfortable
uncooperative
uneasy
unfair

unfeeling
unfriendly
unfulfilled
unhappy
unimportant
uninformed
uninterested
unkind
unloved
unnatural
unpopular
unprepared
unsatisfied
unsafe
unsettled
unsophisticated
unsure
unwanted
unwilling
unworthy
upset
uptight
used
useless

vehement
vengeful
violent
vulnerable

warped
waspish
wasteful
weak
weary
weepy
wicked
wild
wishy-washy
withdrawn
worn out
worried
worthless
wrong
wrung out

zig-zaggy
zonked out

ABOUT THE AUTHORS

PETER H. BUNTMAN, M.S.W., ACSW, licensed clinical social worker, is a psychotherapist in private practice in California. He specializes in working with adolescents and their families. Formerly the president of the Southern California Psychotherapy Association of Orange County, Buntman is a member of the Bioenergetic Society of Southern California. He has been the mental-health consultant to numerous federal, state, and local agencies that deal with adolescent problems. Buntman is co-founder and clinical director of the Institute for Adolescent Studies.

ELEANOR M. SARIS, M.Ed., is president of a national consulting firm specializing in educational communication, where she creates innovative curricula designed to improve relations between teachers, adolescents, and their families. She coordinated Parent Effectiveness and Youth Effectiveness Training Programs throughout southern California. For four years, she was administrative assistant to Dr. Thomas Gordon, author of PARENT EFFECTIVENESS TRAINING. Saris is co-founder and executive director of the Institute for Adolescent Studies.